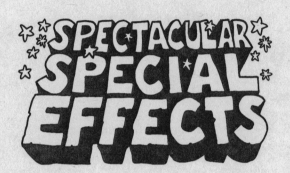

Other titles in the series

The Knowledge

SPECTACULAR SPECIAL EFFECTS

DIANA KIMPTON

Illustrated by
Royston Robertson

Hippo

To Paul – my favourite special effects man

Scholastic Children's Books,
Commonwealth House, 1–19 New Oxford Street,
London WC1A 1NU, UK
a division of Scholastic Ltd
London ~ New York ~ Toronto ~ Sydney ~ Auckland
Mexico City ~ New Delhi ~ Hong Kong

Published in the UK by Scholastic Ltd, 2002

Text copyright © Diana Kimpton, 2002
Illustrations copyright © Royston Robertson, 2002
Cover illustration copyright © Clive Goddard, 2002

ISBN 0 439 99230 3

Typeset by TW Typesetting, Midsomer Norton, Somerset
Printed by Cox & Wyman Ltd, Reading, Berks

2 4 6 8 10 9 7 5 3 1

The right of Diana Kimpton and Royston Robertson to be identified as the
author and illustrator of this work respectively has been asserted by them in
accordance with the Copyright, Designs and Patents Act, 1988.

CONTENTS

INTRODUCTION

What do you think is the most spectacular special effect you've ever seen? Maybe it's the talking pig in *Babe*, the dinosaurs in *Jurassic Park* or the pod race in *The Phantom Menace*.

Or maybe it's one of the effects that are so good you don't realize they are effects at all – scenes where you think the movie makers really have blown up a warehouse or sailed a ship into a hurricane. The selection is so huge that it's impossible to choose.

All those scenes happened in movies but special effects are used on stage too. People have always loved telling stories but as soon as they started to act them out, they ran into trouble. How could a god look as if he came down from the sky? How could you make it look as if you'd killed someone without them ending up dead? How could a very ordinary person look like a scary monster?

Problems like these gave birth to the art of special effects. No one knows for sure when that happened.

Perhaps it was when some highly inventive caveman said...

Since then the monsters have got better and the scenery more spectacular but the basic principle (and the fascination with fog) remains the same. Special effects are about illusion – making people believe in something that isn't there.

Do you want to know how those illusions are done? Do you fancy making collapsing shelves, wilting flowers and buckets of blood? Are you ready to face the challenge of directing *Attack from Planet Hamster*? Then read on and learn the secrets of spectacular special effects.

LANDMARKS IN SPECIAL EFFECTS

5th century AD
The Ancient Greeks use a crane to lower actors playing the gods to the stage. This effect, called *deus ex machina*, is supposed to make them look as if they are coming down from heaven.

15th century
Medieval mystery plays include fire and flood effects as well as occasional dragons for St George to kill.

1610
Shakespeare is awkward enough to demand that one of the characters in *The Winter's Tale* should "exit, pursued by a bear" – thereby creating a challenge for generations of special effects experts.

1862
Professor John Henry Pepper makes a ghost appear on stage when he uses his "Pepper's Ghost" effect for the first time.

1895

Georges Méliès sees moving pictures for the first time – triggering an interest which led him to develop some of the earliest movie effects.

1923

Special effects re-enact the parting of the Red Sea in *The Ten Commandments*.

1927

The arrival of the talkies allows sound effects to make visual ones seem even more believable.

1933

King Kong successfully uses almost all the special effects techniques available at that time including several 45-cm-high models of the great ape, a 6-metre-tall model of its head and shoulders and a mechanical paw large enough to hold actress Fay Wray.

1954

Twenty Thousand Leagues Under the Sea uses a full-size model of a giant squid that weighs several tonnes and needs 16 people to operate it.

1963
The *Dr Who* TV series breaks new ground in using low-budget special effects to make children hide behind the settee.

1968
2001 – A Space Odyssey leaves audiences stunned by both its breathtaking special effects and its incomprehensible plot.

1977
Industrial Light and Magic's effects for *Star Wars* create a whole universe on screen and makes the company famous.

1982
The genesis sequence in *Star Trek II: The Wrath of Khan* uses computer generated images to show the transformation of a barren planet into a living world.

1986
The musical *Phantom of the Opera* combines Victorian

stagecraft with state-of-the-art technology to create effects which include two disappearances, an underwater lake and a reflection that steps out of a mirror.

1988
The first ever on-screen morphing between one picture and another happens in *Willow*.

1993
Digital dinosaurs have starring roles for the first time in *Jurassic Park*.

1995
Computer graphics and animatronics make real animals appear to talk in *Babe*.

1997
Titanic breaks all records with its $200 million budget, a large proportion of which was spent on its special effects.

2000
The success of *Chicken Run* proves there is still a place for stop-motion photography in animated films.

THE MAGIC OF SPECIAL EFFECTS

Special effects is about illusion and, for hundreds of years, the masters of illusion were the magicians. As they experimented with ways to make their tricks work, they worked out many of the principles that are still important to effects today. So let me introduce you to Presto the Implausible who has kindly agreed to let you in on some of the secrets of his profession.

Seeing is believing: or is it the other way round?

Here is a vase. It looks very ordinary and it is. Presto bought it on his way here. It only cost £1 and there were a hundred just like it in the shop. It's boring, isn't it? It certainly doesn't put you in the mood for magic.

13

Now here is another vase. It looks amazingly similar but this one is thousands of years old. It was cunningly crafted by the hands of Mestices, the greatest of all the Egyptian magicians, and woven into its clay is the secret of his magic powers. He took it with him when he was banished from the  kingdom and many thought it had vanished for ever. But his successors have kept it safe, passing it secretly from one magician to another down through the ages until finally it reached Presto – the person legend had decreed should show the world its secrets.

Hopefully by this point, you are enjoying the story and looking forward to seeing what happens next. You want to know the secrets of the vase. You want to see its hidden powers revealed. Although deep down inside you know there is no such thing as real magic, you are ready and willing to be fooled. So Presto has much more chance of impressing you with his skills with this vase than he would have had with the one you saw first (even though they really both came from the same shop).

This is equally true for plays, TV and movies. If the story is good enough, you get so deeply involved with it that you want to believe in its imaginary world even if the scenery wobbles a bit. You stop wondering how the special effects are done and just concentrate on what might happen next. That's one reason why effects in bad films never seem as convincing as those in good ones. If the story doesn't

14

capture your interest, you're much more likely to spot how the visual tricks are done.

∽ Presto's First Principle ∽
If you want to make people believe they are seeing something, first of all make them want to believe it ...

The magic art of misdirection

Have you ever seen an old movie where the hero is face to face with a baddie brandishing a gun? The scene goes something like this...

Which brings us neatly to...

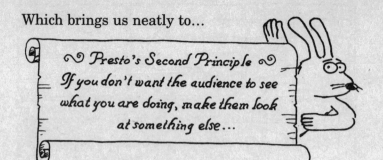

Presto's Second Principle
If you don't want the audience to see what you are doing, make them look at something else...

This is easiest to do when you are making a movie as you have complete control over what pictures appear on the screen. If you don't want the audience to see something, you just don't show it. You can stop the camera and then start it again or cut to a completely different scene for a few seconds.

What the audience saw...

What really happened...

Live performances like Presto's present more of a challenge as most people are far too clever to be caught by the "it's behind you" trick. But there are plenty of other ways to persuade people to look the other way. Here are a few that Presto uses.

Selina the Downright Skinny

Selina is far more than just a pretty girl waiting to be sawn in half. She's a well-rehearsed assistant who moves around the stage, talks and waves things at convenient moments to distract our attention.

The magic wand

In reality, this is only a piece of wood painted black and white. It has no magical powers at all but when Presto waves it around in one hand, we look at it and don't notice what his other hand is doing.

The patter

This is the name magicians give to the words Presto says as he performs his tricks. He may be telling jokes, describing what he's doing or relating a fanciful tale about an Egyptian vase but he keeps talking. And all the time he keeps talking, we keep listening and when we listen to someone, we tend to concentrate on their face rather than their hands.

Flashes

A bright flash on stage attracts our attention in a very dramatic way. It hides what's behind it and dazzles us so it's hard to see anything for a moment.

Black is magic

Black has a certain magical quality which Presto is going to demonstrate with the help of his cat, Cuthbert.

He is probably the blackest cat you have ever seen. He hasn't got a single white hair on his body. Presto will now place Cuthbert in the coal cellar.

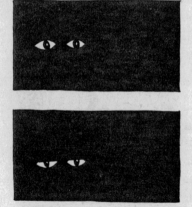

And wait.

And wait...

Which proves that the old saying "You can't see a black cat in a coal cellar" is true, provided the cat is asleep, and brings us neatly to Presto's third principle...

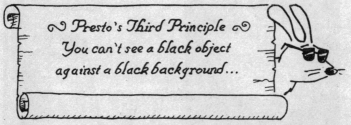

~ *Presto's Third Principle* ~
*You can't see a black object
against a black background...*

Most stages have a black backcloth to help put this principle into practice. This conveniently hides the black wire holding up Presto's not-so-amazing-now-you-know-how-it's-done floating flowerpot.

BLACK
BACKCLOTH

It also hides the person working this ostrich puppet because he is dressed from head to foot in black. To make the effect even better, the ostrich is fluorescent pink which glows in the ultraviolet stage lighting.

Most amazingly of all, the black backcloth can help make a woman appear suddenly in the middle of the stage.

Before her appearance, she stands on stage on a low table or step so her whole body, including her feet, is in front of the black backcloth. She holds a black cloth in front of herself so she is completely hidden and she stays very still. The effect works best if the action on the stage encourages the audience to look away from her and the lighting is arranged so her part of the stage is in shadow.

Suddenly there is a loud drum roll. She drops the cloth and steps forward as a bright spotlight picks her out.

TO MAKE THESE EFFECTS WORK WELL, THE BLACK NEEDS TO BE REALLY BLACK — NOT DARK GREY — AND IT MUSTN'T BE SHINY. BLACK VELVET IS A GOOD CHOICE

ERIC

ERIC, OUR SPECIAL EFFECTS EXPERT

MOVIE MAGIC

The first moving pictures seemed magical to people who had never seen them before. That's hardly surprising, because stage magic is about illusion and movies are the greatest illusion of them all. Nothing we see on screen is really there. We think we are watching dinosaurs, spaceships or explorers in a jungle, but all we are really seeing is coloured lights on a screen.

The people behind the movies

Creating that illusion involves a huge number of people. As well as the producer, director, actors and special effects team, there are designers, camera operators, lighting experts, wardrobe people, set builders, make-up artists, electricians, cleaners, drivers, people who make the sandwiches and loads of others. The list goes on and on.

BUT WE'RE THE MOST IMPORTANT ONES...

Each member of the team contributes their own particular skill to help produce the final product – the strip of film which makes those coloured lights tell a story on the screen.

How movies work

If you look at that film, you'll see a strip of still pictures (called frames), each photographed a short moment after the one before.

The film projector shines each of these pictures one by one on to the screen. If it did this very slowly, you would see each one individually but it doesn't. It shows them so quickly that it moves on to the next picture before the image of the one before has completely faded from your eyes. That makes your brain blend the pictures together so you think you see movement.

The phenomenon that makes this work is called persistence of vision. You can experiment with it yourself by asking a friend to wave a bright torch at you in a dark room. If she does it slowly, you will just see one point of light moving around but if she waves it really fast, the torch will seem to leave a track of light.

AND THEN AS IF BY MAGIC...

YOU CAN'T STOP THERE! IT WAS JUST GETTING INTERESTING

You can also make your own animated cartoon using an exercise book. Draw a series of pictures of a character – one on the bottom right-hand corner of each page. Make the character move slightly from one picture to the next. Don't worry if you can't draw well – a simple stick man is quite good enough. Here are some pictures you can copy if you want to.

Now flip through the corners of the pages and, if you do it at the right speed, you'll see your character move.

If you want to see one the illustrator did earlier, flip the bottom right corner of this book to make Presto's rabbit move.

George Méliès, the movie magician

Almost as soon as moving pictures were invented at the end of the nineteenth century, people started to experiment with trick photography. The best known of these early special effects men lived in France. His name was Georges Méliès and, if you've read the first chapter, you won't be surprised to learn that he was a stage magician.

Méliès fell in love with movies as soon as he saw his first one in 1895. He bought his own camera and at first he just filmed the world around him. Movies were so new that audiences didn't demand a story. They were happy to watch anything – trains, the sea, even films of people playing cards.

Then one day when he was filming in Paris, the film in the camera got stuck. It took him a minute to free it and, of course, while he was doing that the traffic and the people kept moving. When he fixed the camera, he started filming again and, when he developed the film, he saw an amazing sight. A bus appeared to change into a hearse and men changed into women.

This simple accident showed Méliès the camera's potential for producing amazing trickery. From then on, he combined his knowledge of stage magic with these new camera tricks to make special effects movies which delighted his audiences. He sent men to the moon, created giants and took off his own head while he was talking – all with just a heavy, fixed camera and no help from a computer.

Méliès' black magic

Like Presto and all other magicians, Méliès knew how useful black could be. But when he started to experiment with film, he found another use for it.

Film reacts to light. When you take a photograph, the shutter in the camera opens briefly and the light that comes in creates a picture on the film.

If you open the shutter again without moving the film on, you create a second picture over the top of the first one. This is called a double exposure and is usually such a nuisance that most modern cameras have a safety feature to stop you taking one by mistake.

Méliès used the magic of black to make a double exposure look as if both pictures were taken at once. First of all, he would film a scene where one part of the set was completely black.

Black doesn't give off any light so the piece of film in each frame which showed the black area was left unexposed.

Then he ran back the film and filmed another person against a black background which wouldn't affect the film.

He organized this carefully so their picture fitted into the black area of the original scene. If they stood very close to the camera, they looked enormous in comparison with the other people. If they stood well back from the camera, they looked tiny, like this.

One of his most spectacular effects was in a film called *L'Homme à la Tête de Caoutchouc* (he was French, remember – it means *The Man with the Rubber Head*). In it, he used this double exposure technique to produce the effect of a head being pumped up with bellows until it finally exploded. First of all, he filmed the whole scene without the head but with a black area where it would be.

Then he wound back the film and filmed his own head against a black background. He sat in a black box so his body couldn't be seen and the box was pulled towards the camera mounted on a sloping track.

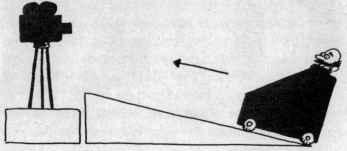

As he got closer and closer to the camera, the picture of his head grew bigger and bigger. The sloping track made sure his head stayed at the same level so it always fitted in the black area of the first picture.

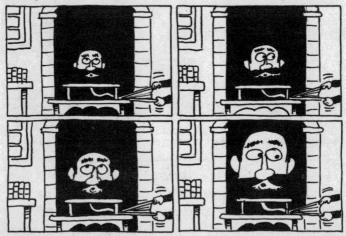

The double exposure made it look as if the head was growing larger because of the bellows.

This effect is even more impressive when you remember Méliès had no computers or other technology to help him. He had to get the second shot right first time or start the whole process over again.

The magic of mattes

Double exposure shots don't always need an area of black in the original scene to make them work. Another way is to put something in front of the camera to stop the light reaching some of the film while you shoot the first scene. Then a corresponding piece stops the light spoiling the first scene while you shoot the second. Each of the shapes used to block the light is called a matte.

The simplest matte is a rectangle and you can experiment with it yourself if you have a still camera which lets you take double exposures.

- First put the rectangle over one half of the lens.

- Take a picture of someone with the other half.

- Don't wind the film on.

- Now put the rectangle over the other half of the lens.

- Use that half of the lens to take a picture of the same person standing to one side of where they were the first time.

- The final picture will look like identical twins.

As technology has improved, the different ways of combining several shots into one picture have become cleverer and cleverer. Black is no longer the important colour. Now a blue or green background is used for individual shots instead. The blue or green can be removed later and the important part of the shot combined with the right background after the actual filming is over.

Nowadays this process is done using computers but, before they were available, it was done by a painstaking process using what are called *travelling mattes* to expose different sections of the film to the light at different times. Suppose you needed to combine this blue-screen shot of a hamster...

...with this shot of a forest.

First you'd use the blue-screen shot of the hamster to make two mattes – a black hamster-shaped silhouette and a black rectangle with a hamster-shaped hole.

Then you'd use the first matte to make a version of the forest shot with a hamster-shaped hole.

Finally you'd use the other matte to cover the picture of the forest while you add the hamster.

The end result makes the hamster look enormous, but the same technique can also make humans look tiny, as they did in *The Borrowers*.

More haste, less speed

Modern film projectors show movies at 24 frames per second. If you film a scene slower than this, the projector will speed up the action. For instance, a two-second shot filmed at 12 frames per second will only take one second to show on screen. This is very useful for action films where cars driving at safe speeds can be made to look as if they are going hair-raisingly fast. Of course, you have to be careful not to have anyone on foot in the shot or the speed of their legs will give the trick away.

If you film your scene at more than 24 frames per second, the projector will slow the action down. For instance, a one-second shot filmed at 240 frames per second will last 10 seconds on screen. This is useful for space-walking scenes and, as we'll find out later, it can be particularly important when you are using model shots.

Back-to-front...

The projector always shows the movie from the beginning to the end but you don't have to film it that way. Suppose you have a battle scene where an arrow has to slam into the wall only millimetres from your hero's head.

Even the most skilled archer in the world can't guarantee to place an arrow that accurately. If it lands just a few millimetres away in the wrong direction, both your hero and your film-directing career could come to an untimely end.

One solution is to film the whole shot backwards. Start with the arrow in the wall and position your hero beside it. Then ask him to act back to front while you pull the arrow out with a piece of string too thin to show up on screen. All you have to do then is reverse the film to get the amazing shot you wanted.

...and sideways

Now imagine you need a shot of someone climbing a mountain but there isn't a convenient one available. An easy solution is to ask them to crawl along the ground, pretending they are climbing, while you film them with the camera turned sideways. When you play the film, the ground will look vertical and they will look as if they are climbing up it.

33

Be careful the background doesn't give it away. You can organize the shot so it can't be seen or arrange bushes or rocks at the right angle behind your climbers. If you were making a high-budget movie, you'd film your climbers in front of a blue screen and then combine them with background shots of a real mountain during post-production.

OOPS!

Cheap effects for empty pockets

Not all special effects cost thousands of pounds. Can you work out what these low-budget ones can be used to portray on stage or screen?

1. Porridge.

2. Shaking the camera while the actors fall about on the set.

3. Cotton wool.

4. A bubble from a piece of bubble wrap filled with custard.

5. Cold tea (without milk).

6. Washing-up gloves painted gold.

7. A solution of Epsom salts in beer.

8. Curry powder.

9. Green pea soup.

10. A Polo mint broken into several pieces.

Answers:

1. This can flow down a model mountain just like lava from a volcano. Adding some food colouring can help it look red hot.

2. This is a brilliant way to film an earthquake cheaply, especially if someone lying on the floor out of shot wobbles the furniture too. You can use the same technique to show an attack on a spaceship – they did it all the time on *Star Trek*.

3. Cotton wool is a traditional substitute for fluffy white clouds in model shots. Model aircraft can fly between them very convincingly but trying to fly them through the cloud gives the trick away.

4. Stuck on an actor with suitable glue and covered with make-up, this becomes a disgustingly squeezable spot. If you're filming a gruesome close-up, make sure there's some glass or plastic in front of the camera to stop the custard getting on the lens.

STAND BACK – THIS COULD GET MESSY

5. Cold tea is a traditional substitute for whisky on both stage and screen. While filming *Gone with the Wind*, Clark Gable played a trick on his leading lady by replacing it with the real thing.

6. Hands for robots as used in *Dr Who* – a TV series that also featured bombs made from lavatory ballcocks with fins attached.

7. When painted on glass and allowed to dry, this looks like frost. Although it's cheap, it's also very effective and has been used on stage and screen for many years.

8. Curry powder makes good sand for models – korma is best for yellow sand and madras for a darker gold. It also gives your models a very interesting smell and can sting if it gets in your eyes, so be careful.

9. This excellent replacement for vomit is runny enough to pump through tubes for really disgusting effects. It was used in the filming of *The Exorcist* to make an actress appear to be so violently sick that it sprayed in all directions. The soup was pumped to an outlet in her mouth through a hidden tube.

10. If an actor spits these out after a fall, they look like broken teeth. This very effective trick is worth remembering next April Fool's Day.

ARE THEY REALLY THERE?

Scriptwriters set their stories in the past, in the future, in every part of the world and sometimes even in galaxies far, far away. The challenge for the set designer and special effects crew is to make the audience believe the actors are really there.

Presto's first principle is very important here, especially with live theatre. The better the plot, the more likely the audience are to let themselves believe the actors are in the country or a cathedral rather than standing on a stage. But it also helps if you can hint at the setting before the scene gets properly under way. In theatre, this is often done with sound effects and music – birdsong and bleating sheep for the country or a tolling bell and hymn to suggest the cathedral.

In a movie, this same effect is achieved with what is called an establishing shot. A brief glimpse of the Golden Gate bridge, the Eiffel Tower or a tropical rainforest helps the audience imagine that is where the next scene is happening. In the same way, a shot of a spooky castle on a mountain top followed by a shot of an equally spooky bedroom makes us believe the bedroom is inside the castle. More spectacularly, a view looking down from the top of a tall building followed by a shot of the hero balanced on a ledge makes us believe he is high above the ground instead of just a metre above the studio floor.

Sets and scenery

There's an old proverb which says "all that glitters is not gold" but deep down inside we don't believe it. Our brains are easily fooled, especially if we want them to be.

If something looks like stone, we assume it *is* stone and if we can see the front of a building, we assume the rest of the building is behind it.

This is extremely useful if you are building a set. It allows you to make rocks light enough to throw without hurting people, transform a stage into the inside of a castle and build a city street out of flat pieces of wood and no bricks.

Fortunately Eric, our resident special effects expert, has volunteered to show you some of the tricks of the trade. Although he is not a magician, he will now transform three incredibly uninteresting pieces of cardboard into incredibly uninteresting pieces of something else.

Transformation no. 1: cardboard into wood

- Paint the cardboard a light wood colour and leave to dry.
- Add the wood grain pattern in a darker wood colour. For small areas on models, you can do this by hand. For large areas, paint the card with the dark wood colour and, while the paint is still wet, spread it into the required pattern with a special wood-graining tool.
- Hey Presto – wood.

Transformation no. 2: cardboard into marble

- Paint the cardboard white.
- While the paint is still wet, drip on very pale grey or brown paint which will spread out to make slightly darker patches in the white.
- When the paint is dry, paint on the distinctive dark veins with a very fine brush.
- Hey Presto – marble.

Transformation no. 3: cardboard into metal

- Paint the cardboard with aluminium wood primer or other metallic paint.
- When the paint is dry, rub dark shoe polish over it.
- Rub off the polish and, because the cardboard is slightly uneven, you'll find some remains in the low places.
- Hey Presto – metal.

This type of magic with paint is particularly useful for making props. Stone, wood and metal are heavy, slow and noisy to move around, so lightweight alternatives made of cardboard, polystyrene and foam are much easier to use. They also cause much less pain when they fall on the actors.

The wonders of polystyrene

Polystyrene is particularly useful as it can be carved into almost any shape the plot demands, but there is a problem. If you think back to the last time you unpacked anything with polystyrene packing, you'll realize it easily breaks into tiny white beads which go everywhere and spoil the illusion of your hero being buried by a rock fall.

Naturally Eric knows a way round this. First he cuts the polystyrene into the shape he wants. Then he coats it with several layers of a very thin cloth called scrim, held on with plenty of PVA glue. The combined effect of the PVA and the scrim protects the polystyrene from breaking and, as an added bonus, makes it less likely to catch fire. So next time you see a rock bounce unconvincingly across an alien landscape, don't think, "Ah ha – polystyrene." Think, "Ah ha – polystyrene, scrim and PVA."

Magic tricks with paintings

Everyone knows stage plays use painted backdrops. However good the artist, there is no way he can fool you completely. You know you're in a theatre. That gorgeous view of Rome, the Alps or beautiful countryside can't be real so it must be a painting.

In the movies, the paintings are much less obvious, but they are still there. Very early movies used backdrops similar to those used in theatre, but the magic of film means there are much more imaginative and convincing ways to use paintings to set the scene.

Glass paintings

These are a wonderful way to turn unexciting locations into the perfect setting for your film. Suppose the plot calls for a palace with towering spires and the only place you can find to film is your local school. Just ask an extremely skilful artist to paint the top half of the palace on a piece of glass, carefully arrange it in front of your camera so the painted building matches up with the real one and then film the shot through it.

Alternatively, suppose you are filming a war movie and you want a shot looking down through the roof of a bombed-out building.

Step 1 Find a flat piece of ground next to a tall building.

Step 2 Put some rubble and pieces of wood around to make the piece of ground look like the inside of the building.

Step 3 Go to a high enough floor in the building to get the shot you want.

Step 4 Film the shot through a piece of glass with the remains of the roof painted on it or, better still, through a model of the roof.

Matte paintings

A more common way to use paintings is to combine them with the live action after it's been filmed.

Imagine you're directing a film where a terrified bystander has to run up a hill away from an alien spaceship full of giant hamsters. Unfortunately, there isn't a real spaceship available and the budget

43

won't run to a full-scale replica so you have a problem. Stephen Spielberg had a similar one when his hero had to walk towards a non-existent native village in *Indiana Jones and the Temple of Doom*. Spielberg used a matte painting to solve his problem and so can you. The technique works like this...

First film the actor running up the hill.

Now ask an artist to paint a picture of the spaceship to fit in with the hill. (He needn't worry about the hamsters – they are all inside.)

In post-production, combine the two together in the same shot.

In the past, this was done using mattes to expose only part of the film at a time, but nowadays the two pictures are combined using a computer.

Matte paintings can also save Eric building huge sets. He just builds the small section that the director needs for the live action and an artist paints the rest. So this...

...becomes this...

Stephen Spielberg used this technique to film the Ark of the Covenant being hidden in a vast warehouse at the end of *Raiders of the Lost Ark*.

First he filmed a man with a forklift truck in a small area of shelving. Then, in post-production, he added that shot to a painting of a huge warehouse to make the memorable final scene.

Moving backgrounds

Painted backgrounds never move and neither do the huge still photographs which are sometimes used in their place. This doesn't matter with pictures of buildings or distant mountains, but some shots like street scenes need movement in them to be convincing. One way to add this type of background to a studio shot is to film the scene in advance and then project it on to a large screen behind the actors.

Sometimes the film is projected on to the back of the screen – a process called rear projection.

The alternative is to project the film on to the front of the screen. To stop the projector getting in the way of the camera, movie makers use a special technique called front projection. They put the projector on one side and project the picture on to a two-way mirror. The mirror reflects the picture on to a special screen while the camera sees through the mirror to film the shot.

Both these methods of combining actors with filmed footage let the director see what the finished shot will look like while he is filming.

Blue-screen shots

Filming actors in front of a blue or green screen allows their action to be combined with a painted, filmed or computer-generated background in post-production. It can even make live actors appear in a cartoon as they did in *Who Framed Roger Rabbit* and *Mary Poppins*. Each shot has to be carefully planned in advance as the director can't see what the finished image will look like while he is filming the action.

Paint problems

One big problem with painted scenery and photographs is that they only look perfect when viewed straight on. If you look at one slightly sideways, you realize it's a picture because your view of the houses or trees doesn't change.

THIS PUTS THE PROBLEM INTO PERSPECTIVE

Fortunately that doesn't mean you have to build the whole set or find the perfect location for shots where a painting won't work. There's another alternative – build a model.

But before we look at models, there's one more "are they really there?" problem to think about – crowd scenes.

Two's company, three's a crowd

Exciting scripts often include attacking armies, rebel hordes or huge crowds of onlookers, but large numbers of actors in a production can cause a number of problems.

1. They all want to be paid, which stretches the budget.

2. They all have to wear costumes, which stretches the wardrobe.

3. It's hard to make them all do what you want, when and where you want it, which stretches the director's temper.

One way round this is to cheat.

Another is to have the actors march past in a long line with the ones at the front running round to join the back as soon as they are out of sight of the audience.

But the special effects department can come up with some other solutions.

Using computer graphics

The computer's ability to copy and paste a picture many times can build very convincing crowds from a small number of actors. It's a more sophisticated version of the people marching round in circles technique and it has the same problem – unless it's done very carefully the audience may spot that many people in the crowd look the same.

Sometimes directors want to use this to add a spooky feel to the story. Otherwise they can avoid it by:

- Photographing each actor several times in different clothes.

- Having the crowd so far away that the individual faces are blurred.

- Only giving the audience brief glimpses of the crowd.

A full-size puppet army

This technique works on stage provided all the soldiers are marching. The audience may spot the trick but, if they do, they'll just be amazed at how clever it is.

Each actor has two full-size puppets, one on either side, which are very realistic and dressed to fit in with the rest of the cast. These are attached to a framework he wears on his back like a rucksack. Strings attached to his arms and legs make the puppets move in the same way that he does.

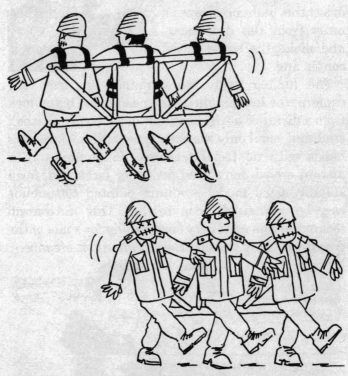

Dummies, cut-outs and cotton buds
Dummies and cut-out figures can be very effective substitutes for people who don't have to move – guards on castle battlements, soldiers on parade or a crowd listening to a speech. The further away they are, the more likely they are to fool the audience, so

it often works well to have live actors at the front of the crowd with the dummies or cut-outs at the back. Also, one or two live actors among the stuffed ones will add some movement to draw the audience's eyes away from the dummies and make the scene more convincing.

THE GENTLE ART OF MISDIRECTION AGAIN

The further away the dummies are from the camera, the less detailed they need to be. If you look from a distance at the back row of a crowded football stadium, you'll only see the vague outline of people's heads with no facial features. So dummies in a distant crowd don't need bodies or faces and, for a suitably-sized model stadium, painted cottonbuds can be amazingly convincing. This cottonbud technique was used very successfully for some of the crowd watching the pod race in *Phantom Menace*.

YOU'RE CLEANING YOUR EAR WITH MY FAVOURITE CHARACTER!

It's also a useful reminder of the importance of models in movie making. So let's take a better look at this vital part of special effects.

MODEL MAGIC

Do you need a Death Star to attack the rebel forces? Do you want a bicycle to fly through the sky carrying a small boy and a lost alien? Do you need some far less friendly aliens to blow up the White House?

Movie making is full of challenges like these – scenes that would be impossible, too dangerous or too expensive to film for real.

The solution for all those problems and many others is to build models. These are sometimes called miniatures, but that name can be misleading. Models for special effects vary enormously in size and some of them are huge. Although a model building for one shot may be only a few centimetres high, a model of the same building for a different shot may be taller than a man.

Why model shots work

The size of the pictures in a movie depends on the size of the screen, not the size of the objects in real life. So, one minute the screen may be filled with Gloria Lovealot's face, the next with Barry the Hamster and the next with a 20-tonne truck.

53

As you watch the film, you instantly believe that everything is the size you would expect it to be in real life. That's partly because your brain assumes everything is normal unless something makes it think otherwise. But it's also because, without realizing it, you've used clues in the pictures to help judge the sizes – so you've compared Gloria to the glass, Barry to the water bottle and the truck to the tree.

Now, suppose Barry gets bored and wanders off into the next shot.

Suddenly your brain has a problem to tackle. This picture isn't one you would usually expect to see so you've got to decide if you're watching…

a) *Attack from Planet Hamster*, or

b) *Barry the Hamster meets Timmy the Toy Truck*.

Your brain looks for any clue which can throw new light on the dilemma and, in particular, searches for other objects to help judge how big the two main characters are.

If we put a flower or two beside Barry, it must be the Toy Truck film.

But if we put the tree back and maybe add a house, it's time to hide behind a cushion and scream.

Now let's pull you out of the audience and put you back into the role of film director. The script demands an attack by a giant hamster, but none have turned up for audition. Your only hope is to use your own favourite pet (who is a bit overweight but not exactly enormous) and a model truck. How can you make the attack convincing enough to fool the audience?

First of all, you need to realize that you'll never fool them completely. Everyone knows there is no such thing as a giant hamster (move your ear, Barry, you're blocking out the light) but audiences watch movies ready to be entertained. They happily put their sense of disbelief into cold storage and go along with whatever they see on screen provided there is nothing there which makes them doubt it.

MY FIRST PRINCIPLE...

...AGAIN

You've got no problem making the hamster look realistic, but it will only look large enough if the truck and the surrounding scenery is convincing. The more detailed the model, the more chance you have of persuading the audience that it's real.

You can increase that chance with several techniques that all film directors love.

Make sure the audience can't see the model very well

If they can't see it properly, they won't spot what's wrong. This explains why movie monsters so often attack at night or in thick fog. Driving rain can have a similar effect, but it's a less popular choice as it can wreak havoc with electrical connections.

Make sure the audience can't see the model for too long

A quick glimpse of the truck, followed by a shot of a giant paw crashing through the windscreen is far more convincing than a long lingering shot of the hamster on the truck. If the shot has to be longer, keep the camera moving so it doesn't focus on any single part of the model for too long.

Add live action to the shot

If you can add some tiny people running away screaming, they will make the shot look more authentic. Their size will help the hamster look enormous and their movement will draw the audience's eyes away from the truck and the scenery. One way to do this is to film them in front of a blue screen and then add them to the main shot in post-production.

But there is another way which doesn't require any technology, although it does need some very clever model building and a lot of space. It relies on perspective – the effect which makes things a long way away look much smaller than they really are.

- First build your model set with a gap in the back.
- Find some actors (the shorter the better) and stand them behind the gap, far enough away that they look the right size beside the truck.
- Put some scenery around your actors which blends in with the scenery on your model set.
- Now start filming and tell your actors to run away screaming. If you've done everything right, they will look as if they are on your model set.

Making models ... and cutting the grass

Making models for special effects takes skill, patience and the willingness to see something you have laboured over for weeks blown apart in seconds. That's because much of the destruction we

58

see on screen is achieved with models. Few films have budgets large enough to allow them to destroy real helicopters, and trying to blow up the White House or the Houses of Parliament is likely to get you arrested.

Models take a long time to make, so model makers are always happy to find short cuts. Provided the scale is right, ordinary doll's house furniture inside a specially-built model building can add authenticity when it explodes. Plastic model kits can yield useful details for the outside of space ships, toothpaste tube tops can become tiny flower pots; and, with a bit of ingenuity, table-tennis balls can become anything from puppet eyes to alien planets.

It's often the little details which take the time. When *The Avengers* movie was being filmed, one model shot involved an underground explosion where viewers would see the ripple of the blast spreading across the ground like a ripple on a pond. As the ground was covered with grass, the model had to be too, so several people worked for days and days cutting artificial grass down to the right size with scissors. It was a frustrating job made all the more frustrating when the finished shot was cut from the final movie ... but that's a situation everyone working in the movies has to get used to.

Filming models

As with all special effects, part of the success of a model shot depends on the way it is filmed. Camera angles and lighting can do a great deal to make the model look more authentic and skilled cutting can hide the joins between the model shots and the real ones.

Giving the impression of distance

If you look at distant mountains or buildings, they don't look as clear as objects which are closer to you. If you build a model of the same view and film it with ordinary lighting, the mountains will look crystal clear and give away the fact that they are not real.

In order to make the model shot realistic, the effects team have to give those mountains the same misty quality they would have in real life. One way to do this is to use a small amount of smoke from a smoke machine. Another way is to put some fine gauze or netting between the camera and the mountains. Everything seen through the gauze looks slightly misty.

Making movement look realistic

Because models are smaller than their real-life counterparts, they don't always move in a convincing way. A model car driven off a model cliff only has a short distance to fall so it hits the ground too quickly. An explosion spreads from one end of a 10-cm ship to the other far quicker than it will on a 200-metre one, and small waves move so much faster than large ones that they scream "model shot" to the audience unless you are very careful.

The solution is to slow the action down – and that means filming it at a higher speed than the standard 24 frames per second at which it will be projected. The exact speed depends on the size of the model in relation to real life.

61

Suppose our scene in *Attack from Planet Hamster* ends with the lorry and the hamster plunging over a conveniently-placed cliff. We'll use a model shot with a stuffed stand-in for Barry which takes one second to hit the ground. If we film it at 240 frames per second, that fall will last for 10 seconds in the movie and look much more realistic as a result.

Filming at these high speeds means each frame of film is only exposed to the light for a very short amount of time. This means the light must be very, very bright to produce a high-quality picture. But lighting that bright also produces a lot of heat which can melt plastic and blister paint. When making this type of shot, the effects team can only have all the lights on during the actual filming, or heat will ruin the model before they've had time to use it.

Special effects challenge

At the end of *Attack from Planet Hamster*, the hamster mother ship sucks the remaining hamsters into the air. Animal welfare rules prevent you using real animals and a vacuum cleaner. Can you think how to use a model to do this effect without hurting any hamsters?

Answer: One solution is to build an upside-down model of the set and attach the model hamsters to the upside-down ground with easily removable pegs so they don't fall off. Put an upside-down mother ship at the bottom. Now pull out the pegs so the model hamsters fall into it while you film them with a high-speed camera.

Another technique is to film the model hamsters being dropped out of the mother ship and then reverse the film. Unfortunately, the shot would be spoiled if any of the hamsters bounced, landed upside down or impaled themselves nose first in the ground, so you would probably have to do many takes before you got it right.

But the great thing about special effects is there is no ultimate right answer. Maybe you thought of something better.

Having mastered models, it's now time to look at another major task for the effects team – making weather.

WORKING WONDERS WITH WEATHER

Weather often plays an important part in plots but the real thing rarely co-operates with film makers and can't be used at all on stage. So making weather is an important part of special effects and is sometimes called "atmospherics".

Fog

Fog is one of the great aids to special effects. It adds atmosphere, shows up light beams and hides everything from trailing cables to missing scenery.

There are two main types of fog available. The first is made from frozen carbon dioxide, or "dry ice" as it is more commonly called. When this thaws, it produces a thick mist of water vapour mixed with carbon dioxide which is heavier than air so it sinks down to form a layer close to the ground.

The second is produced by a chemical (often oil or glycerine) in a specially designed smoke machine or sometimes, on outdoor shots, by the same type of smoke canisters used by the army. It spreads around in the same way as real fog or smoke without hugging the ground like dry ice.

It's very important to understand the difference, or an atmospheric dance scene like this…

...can turn into a dramatic portrayal of a pea soup fog.

It's also important not to use too much dry ice to prevent this...

Smoke can be very useful in outdoor shots to give the impression of morning mist in a romantic scene or of cannon fire in a battle. However, it blows around easily so a sudden change in wind direction can cause big problems.

Wind

Electric fans mean wind is the easiest of the elements to produce to order. An ordinary domestic one can add a realistic breeze to a model shot, but much larger, specially designed ones called wind machines are used for normal film work.

TURN IT DOWN!

Rain

Have you ever noticed that rain in movies is always incredibly heavy? That's not only because it's more dramatic than drizzle, it's because it's more noticeable. Light rain just doesn't show up on screen.

In theory, it's possible to add falling rain electronically to a shot in post-production but it doesn't fool the audience because it doesn't make people wet. So the usual way to make rain for the screen is by spraying water into the air so it falls down over the actors. An ordinary hose pipe works for close-ups but attachments called rain heads make hoses work better over larger areas. The addition of a wind machine can turn an ordinary downpour into driving rain.

The biggest problem with rain is that it's not only the actors that get wet. You need to protect all the electrical equipment and make sure the rain doesn't trickle down the camera lens. Any props need to be waterproof too or they may disintegrate at a crucial moment.

The wetness problem makes rain really difficult on stage. It's best to suggest it is happening out of sight with the actors coming on wet as if they've just stepped in from a downpour. You can use sound effects to give the impression of rain falling and, if you must show the rain, you can use a rain bar over a doorway like this:

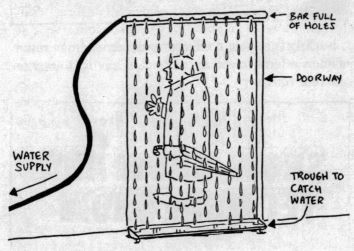

Snow

Snow is vital in many movies. It adds atmosphere to Christmas stories, reality to Arctic ones and allows James Bond to ski dramatically across the mountains pursued by armed gunmen who couldn't hit the side of a barn two metres away. However, although it's fun, real snow can create problems.

- It's not always available, especially in summer.
- It melts under film lights.
- It's slippery.
- It shows footprints which gives away the fact that this is your tenth attempt at filming the first person to arrive at the South Pole.

Luckily the special effects team have a huge range of snow effects to call on instead of having to rely on the real thing.

CAST LIST

Dendritic Salt A favourite years ago as its large crystals look good and crunch realistically underfoot. Now only used with extreme caution as it damages the environment.

Chipped Ice Made by a snow machine from blocks of ice. Looks very good close up but melts to produce water which can be difficult indoors.

Paper snow Looks good, doesn't melt, biodegradable.

Plastic snow Not biodegradable. Clearing up is hard work on location, so more suitable for studio shots.

Starch snow Developed for environmentally sensitive areas, but can be slippery or sticky when wet.

Foam Cheap and fast to lay. Not convincing close up so best for background snow.

Computer Graphics Useful for adding snow on roofs and other inaccessible places during post-production. Can also add steamy breath to scenes filmed in a warm studio.

Which snow they decide to use depends on where they are filming, how long the set will be used for and how much they can afford to spend. Covering the ground with white sheeting before they lay the snow cuts down the amount they need and makes clearing up easier.

Most movie snow scenes use several different snow effects at once and often combine model shots and filmed locations to give the feel of a large area of snow. In the final part of *The X Files Movie*,

Mulder and Scully are in a snowy wasteland. These scenes combined film of a real glacier with green-screen shots of the actors filmed on a studio set with artificial snow in the background and chipped ice in the foreground. The set had refrigeration to keep the ice from melting too quickly under the studio lights, plus a constant supply of fresh ice to repair the set between takes and drainage to carry away the melt water.

Now you've sorted out your scenery, models and weather, it's time to add some action. So let's gather together a hero, a heroine and a bunch of villains for...

THE BIG FIGHT

> **Script**
> Hans um Hunk and Gloria Lovealot are having a meal in a restaurant. They lean forward across the table as if to kiss when (thankfully) three of the Hamsters' human henchmen attack Hans. One hits Hans with a chair which smashes into pieces. Hans leaps to his feet, chases his attacker up the stairs and throws him against the banisters, which break, letting him crash down on to the restaurant floor.

You must have seen scenes like that dozens of times. They happen in nearly every action film and making them involves special props designed to break exactly when required without hurting anyone.

First let's look at that chair. If it was real, it would be Hans's head that broke, not the furniture. What's needed instead is a lightweight chair with very weak joints so it falls apart easily at the right moment. You could make it from balsawood, which is very light, or from cleverly painted foam or polystyrene.

The banisters are another prop. Real ones are strong enough to stop people falling through them but that wouldn't be exciting enough for this scene. Instead, you need specially prepared banisters where the wood has been sawn through at the points where you want them to break and then held together with very weak balsawood dowels. These will be strong enough not to fall over if someone just touches them, but the force of someone falling on them will smash them apart.

THE "BROKEN" BANISTER

BALSAWOOD DOWEL

MATCHING HOLE

PUSH TOGETHER AND THEY WILL HOLD UNTIL SOMEBODY FALLS AGAINST THEM...

Meanwhile, back in the restaurant...

> The remaining two attackers rush towards Hans. Gloria springs to his defence and hits one of them over the head with a huge vase. The vase shatters and the man crumples to the ground.

Most large vases won't break into a thousand pieces when you hit them, unless you use something really hard like a hammer. They are much more likely to just chip or crack, which isn't dramatic enough for this scene. The vases and bottles you see shatter on screen are specially made from light, easily broken materials. Wax works well and is very light, but it isn't as clear as glass and it softens under hot lighting. A better but more expensive solution is a special resin which is light, safe and looks like glass.

If you need real pottery vases, cups and plates to break when they hit the floor, break them beforehand with a hammer and stick them together with very, very weak glue which comes apart on impact. This can keep down the props budget on a stage play as you can stick all the pieces together again between performances.

Meanwhile, back at the restaurant, once more…

> Hans and the only attacker left standing have a dramatic fist fight, taking blow after blow until Hans finally hits the man so hard that he crashes through the plate-glass window into the street.

Of course, the actors aren't really hitting each other. Their blows are carefully worked out beforehand so that each one only touches very gently or misses in such a way that the camera makes it look as if it connects. So when you think you see this…

…what often happens is this…

Falling through a closed window is a very dramatic effect, but even a stunt man wouldn't want to do it with real glass. It would be much too dangerous. The old-fashioned way to do it is with sugar glass – a fake glass made by boiling sugar to a high temperature and then spreading the molten sugar out on a flat surface. The end result is a thin sheet of rock candy – it's not quite as clear as glass, very fragile, attractive to ants and prone to get sticky.

The modern alternative is the same resin used to make fake bottles. This is very clear but not as strong as glass, which is why it breaks easily. Unfortunately, that means it easily breaks when you are putting it in the window, so you need to handle it with great care. The larger the sheet of fake glass, the more difficult it is to handle. That's why people often crash through windows that look like this...

...rather than this...

If you haven't any fake glass, you can give the audience the impression someone's gone through the window without actually showing it. One possible way is like this:

- SHOT 1 -
MAN FALLS BACK FROM BLOW

- SHOT 2 -
CLOSE-UP OF SCREAMING WITH SOUND OF BREAKING GLASS

- SHOT 3 -
SHOT OF BROKEN WINDOW — USE CLEAR PERSPEX CUT TO SHAPE FOR THE GLASS

Collapsing props

Sometimes you don't want a prop to break. You just want it to collapse at the right moment. Wires and strings are a good way of making this type of effect work well.

> The man who fell through the banisters struggles to his feet and lunges at our hero. Hans pushes him back against the wall. The villain slides down and crumples into a sitting position at the bottom. Just at that moment, the shelf above him collapses, showering him with boxes and jars.

The boxes and jars are, of course, extremely light. The shelf is specially made to collapse to order like this.

MAKE A LIGHTWEIGHT SHELF, LIKE THIS

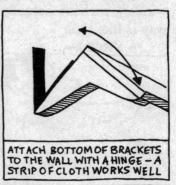

ATTACH BOTTOM OF BRACKETS TO THE WALL WITH A HINGE — A STRIP OF CLOTH WORKS WELL

EYE SCREWED IN WALL

WALL

ATTACH STRING TO TOP OF SHELF AND RUN IT THROUGH AN EYE IN THE WALL SO THAT WHEN PULLED TIGHT, IT PULLS THE SHELF INTO POSITION (A LARGE SHELF MAY NEED MORE THAN ONE PIECE OF STRING)

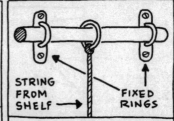

STRING FROM SHELF

FIXED RINGS

RUN STRING TO A CONVENIENT PLACE OUT OF SIGHT AND TIE A RING TO THE END. HOLD STRING TIGHT BY PUTTING A BAR THROUGH THE RING AND TWO OTHER FIXED RINGS

WHEN YOU PULL OUT THE BAR, THE STRING WILL GO SLACK AND THE SHELF WILL COLLAPSE. STACK THE SHELF WITH LIGHT, EMPTY BOXES TO MAKE IT MORE DRAMATIC AND HIDE THE STRING

> Hans nonchalantly brushes the dust from his trousers and leads Gloria from the restaurant. Before he leaves, he pours his untouched glass of wine on to a nearby flower in a pot. The flower droops - the hamsters had poisoned the wine.

For this classic prop you need:

- a piece of plastic tubing painted green
- a stiff wire thin enough to go inside the tubing
- a flower (fake or real)
- a flower pot

1. Cut a piece of tubing long enough to be the flower stem.

2. Push the wire into the tubing. It needs to run the full length of the stem with enough hanging out the end to go down *through* the flower pot.

3. Put the flower on the end of the tubing.

4. Stick the tubing in the flower pot so the wire sticks out through the bottom.

5. Pull the wire down and the flower will droop.

6. To use this prop on

stage, stand it so someone can hide underneath to pull the wire.

WATER, WATER EVERYWHERE

Water is notoriously difficult to film and can easily drive a director to the brink of despair.

The Director's Helpline

Dear Auntie Muriel,

The large quantity of water in my latest film is causing me more trouble than all the other actors put together. Despite all our attempts to keep it in one place, it still escapes through the tiniest hole and delights in getting inside the cameras.

Its ability to conduct electricity is truly shocking and its lack of acting ability is a nightmare, especially in model shots. It seems totally incapable of making small waves behave in the same way as large ones, so even filming in slow motion doesn't solve the problem completely.

But worst of all, it refuses to make any attempt to get on with the rest of the cast. It seems to delight in making them feel wet, cold and – when allowed unrestricted access to their airways – dead.

Please help me.

Yours desperately,

A Worried Director

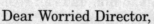

Dear Worried Director,
Please don't take this behaviour personally. All directors find water very difficult to work with. Fortunately, I have just found this wonderful book called *Spectacular Special Effects*. I recommend you read the chapter on water to see how other people cope, and try to arrange for your next movie to be set in a desert.
Yours reassuringly,

Auntie Muriel x

Tanks aren't just for goldfish

Scenes of people in lakes, rivers or the sea are often filmed at the studio in large tanks of water shallow enough to stand up in. So the man in this shot...

...is really perfectly safe.

For added realism, a wind machine and a wave-generating machine can create a very convincing storm in a tank. Alternatively, an outboard motor out of shot can churn the water up to give the impression of a turbulent river.

As its title suggests, the film *Perfect Storm* involved a huge number of storm effects. Although much of the turbulent water was added by computer, the close shots were taken using a full-size replica of a sword-fishing boat in the biggest indoor tank ever created. The boat could be made to rock convincingly while big rollers made waves, artifical rain poured down and water cannons and cascades of water from dump tanks poured over the boat and the actors.

Mermaids and submarines

A deeper tank or swimming pool is useful for underwater shots involving people. If it has glass sides, the camera crew can film without getting wet, but filming inside the tank involves special waterproof cameras and cameramen who can use scuba equipment. To give the impression that someone like a mermaid can breathe underwater, filming has to be divided into very small sections with the actor breathing from an aqualung between takes. This type of filming is very specialized as it can be dangerous, so it uses specially trained crew and actors.

Another way to film underwater shots is not to use water at all. Model shots of submarines can look very effective using smoke and carefully arranged lighting instead. The underwater scenery in *Phantom Menace* was filmed this way, with the submarine and sea creatures added later in post-production.

Of course, if you are doing some really low-budget filming with your dad's video camera, you can try filming through a fish tank ... but it's not very convincing.

WELCOME TO MY UNDERSEA WORLD

Setting sail

You've probably seen movies with really unconvincing model shots of ships which look like a toy ship floating in the bath. It's that water problem again – small waves just don't look like large ones.

The most effective way of filming a boat or ship is to film a real one or a full-size replica on open water. That way it will look really authentic, but it leaves you totally dependent on the weather. The appearance of the sea can change dramatically in only a short period of time, which can make it difficult to link scenes together ... and make you lose your lunch over the side.

If you decide to use a model shot, make the model as large as the size of your budget and the size of the tank will allow. The larger the model, the more it will look like the real thing, especially if you film at high speed and slow it down for the audience.

A third option is to use a model ship but add the water with a computer. Computer-generated water is getting better all the time, so the more techniques improve, the more feasible this solution becomes. If you want to be really clever it's even possible to use a computer-generated ship.

That sinking feeling

Sinking ships are dramatic and dangerous so it's hardly surprising that they are in so many films. The sea battle scene in *Ben Hur* involves a Roman galley sinking. The first silent version of the film used a full-size replica with 400 people on board. On the day it was to catch fire and sink, all the extras were asked if they could swim, but some were so keen to be in the movie that they lied. As a result, the scenes of panic on board as the ship sank didn't involve much acting and the rescue boats were kept busy hauling non-swimmers out of the water.

By the time the next version was made in 1959, the movie industry had become much more safety conscious. The whole sea battle scene was made using models, so no one risked drowning. The model shots were interspersed with studio shots filmed on full-size sets of parts of the ships.

When he filmed *Jaws*, Stephen Spielberg decided to avoid the problems of model shots by filming all the boat scenes at sea. For the final sinking of the shark-hunter's boat, the effects team made a replica boat with tanks underneath. Filling these with compressed air or water gave them control over whether the boat floated or sank so the sinking scene could be repeated again and again until everyone was satisfied with the final shot.

Titanic
The most famous shipwreck in history happened when the ocean liner, *Titanic*, sank on its maiden voyage in 1912 after it hit an iceberg. This disaster provided the inspiration for the film *Titanic*, whose $200 million budget made it one of the most expensive movies ever made. The special effects were one reason for the expense – as well as plenty of digital effects, they involved some very wet actors, computer-generated water, real water on full-size sets and smoke for the underwater scenes.

For the live action shots, James Cameron, the director, ordered the construction of a full-scale but slightly shorter replica of the original ship, correct in every detail except that to save time and money, they only built half of it. The half they built was the right-hand side, but some of the scenes were supposed to take place on the left-hand side. In particular, the ship had to be tied up in Southampton Docks with her left-hand side against the quay.

So, let's put your special effects skills to the test. If you'd been James Cameron, how would you have got round the problem?

His solution was to use some camera magic. He filmed the scenes using the right-hand side of the ship and then turned the film over so the audience saw the mirror image of the original. (This process is called "flopping".) Of course, that could have led to the hero and heroine setting sail in the great ship ɔinɒtiT so the set builders had to make special back-to-front signs and notices to make sure they looked right on screen.

The ship was built in sections. The middle section was built so it could be raised up and down for scenes where the boat is actually going down into the water and the back section could tilt to make it

FROM NOW ON, I ONLY DO FILMS SET IN THE DESERT!

look as if the ship was sinking. To make the tilt look dramatic, stuntmen had to slide down it, looking as if they were falling to their deaths in the sea. To stop them really hurting themselves, the capstans and other hard objects they might hit were made of foam painted to look solid.

For the inside scenes, the set was lowered slowly into a tank of water so the water ran in just as it would in a sinking ship. Between takes, it was lifted up again, dried and reorganized while the actors got dry, put on fresh make-up and dressed in dry clothes.

Some scenes needed the water to look more dramatic. One in particular involves a door giving way to release a torrent of water which surges down a corridor, sweeping away a man carrying a child. To give this effect, thousands of litres of water were dumped suddenly into one end of the corridor from huge containers out of sight of the camera. The man was a stuntman and the child was a dummy.

WE'VE DESTROYED THE ENTIRE SET — PLEASE TELL ME YOU DIDN'T HAVE THE LENS-CAP ON

Another dramatic scene is the moment when the water finally broke through the glass dome of the Grand Staircase. This could have been done with a small model, but it would have been expensive to build one, the problems with filming water might have made it look less than convincing and no one needed the Grand Staircase set any more anyway. So the special effects team dumped thousands of litres of water on to the real set in a one-chance-only effect which completely wrecked the Grand Staircase set.

WARNING
Do not try this at home or you may seriously damage your relationship with your parents.

In *Titanic*, the water was the great threat. It was hard to film and to control but the effects team didn't have to create it from scratch. But stories involving monsters and aliens from other planets present a whole new set of challenges.

MAKING MONSTERS

There are thousands and thousands of different forms of life on Earth. Only a very small number of those are the same shape as us and we are the only ones who walk all the time on our hind legs.

It would be reasonable to expect an even greater diversity of life in the whole universe, but TV and movies constantly depict alien life-forms as the same basic shape as us with just a few extra feelers, arms or eyes. This isn't because they have a greater knowledge of creation than we have. It's just that the easiest way to produce an alien is to dress up an actor.

Some programmes make no real attempt to disguise this fact. Although the make-up is incredibly good and takes hours to put on, many of the aliens in *Star Trek* are just humans with strange faces.

But that isn't suitable for many plots. Aliens and monsters who look completely different from us are far more convincing and far more threatening. Maybe that's why Doctor Who's most feared opponents were the Daleks, despite the fact their plot to take over the universe would have failed completely the first time they met a flight of stairs.

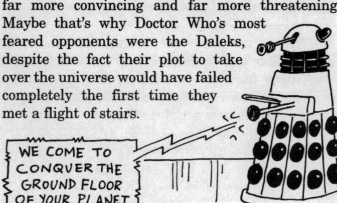

WE COME TO CONQUER THE GROUND FLOOR OF YOUR PLANET

Not all movie and TV monsters have been so successful. Many were so obviously a man in a suit that audiences laughed rather than screamed. But others have worked surprisingly well. Although they weren't monsters in the true sense, the apes in *Planet of the Apes* were very believable and the ones created for *Greystoke: The Legend of Tarzan, Lord of the Apes* looked just like real animals.

So how can you avoid your monster looking like a man dressed up?

Trick 1 *Don't let the audience see your monster at all*
Heavy breathing, looming shadows and the occasional shot of a clawed hand dragging a victim away can be far more scary than an unconvincing monster costume.

Trick 2 *Use an unusually shaped actor*
Not everyone in the world is standard shape. Using an actor who is unusually tall, very small or looks unusual in some other way can help create an alien with a difference – a trick used successfully for the Ewoks in *Return of the Jedi* and Sil, an alien with no legs in *Dr·Who*.

Trick 3 *Use more than one person*
Once you have more than one person inside a monster, you lose the restriction of only being

able to have two legs and two arms. Two people working like this...

YOU'VE GOT TO START AT THE BOTTOM AS AN ACTOR...

...can create a four-legged monster. However, the way it moves is so comical that it's best suited to pantomimes and spoof horror films. This is definitely not an ideal method for creating terrifying giant hamsters.

If the same two people stand very close together, you can create a monster with four realistically waving arms. This technique was used in some shots of the alien queen in *Alien Resurrection* but you could also use it for a giant spider.

Trick 4 *Design the costume to disguise the fact someone is inside*

Suppose you want to make a monster that looks like this...

...from an actor that looks like this...

First put lots of foam padding round the actor's tummy to give him a fat body, some on his shoulders to make him taller and some more round his legs to fatten him up.

The monster's arms are much longer than your actor's, so give him some arm extensions to hold. His wrists will be the monster's elbows.

Now dress him in the monster bodysuit. The bottom of the bodysuit comes down lower than the actor's bottom, which makes his legs look shorter. (Don't overdo this or he won't be able to walk.)
Finally, complete

DOES IT SUIT ME?

your monster by adding the monster's head. This can be a fibreglass frame covered with cloth, latex or silicon and supported on your actor's shoulders. The monster's eyes and mouth are operated by remote control by someone off-stage.

IT'S A BIT HOT IN HERE

Of course, it's important that he can see where he's going.

EXCUSE ME, IS THIS THE FILM STUDIO?

In some costumes, the actor can see out through the monster's eyes or open mouth, but that doesn't work here. Instead, you can put a hole in the neck for him to look through. If you cover this with netting coloured to match the costume, the audience won't spot the hole because it's dark inside the costume and light outside. (To test this, try looking through a net curtain from the light side to the dark side.)

Sometimes even this solution isn't possible and technology is the only answer. Ludo, the huge, gentle monster in *Labyrinth*, had a video camera in one of his horns so the person inside could look at a screen to see where he was going.

Although these tricks are useful, they don't completely take away the restrictions of the human shape. If you want the freedom to create any monster or alien you like, you need to move beyond the actor-in-a-costume technology to the worlds of stop-motion, computer-generated images (CGI) and animatronics.

Introducing stop-motion

Stop-motion animation works on exactly the same principle as cartoon animation, but instead of drawing a sequence of pictures, you take a series of still photographs of models. It's the method behind *Chicken Run* as well as many children's programmes like *Pingu* and, for a long time, it was the only way to show realistic monsters in a movie.

The first step in stop-motion is to make a model creature which can be bent into different shapes – foam on a metal skeleton works well. To make the creature open its mouth and roar:

Step 1 Take a photograph of it.

Step 2 Open its mouth a tiny bit.

Step 3 Take another photograph.

Step 4 Open its mouth a tiny bit more.

Keep repeating these steps until the movement is complete. This can take a long time – it takes 24 individual pictures to make just one second of animation.

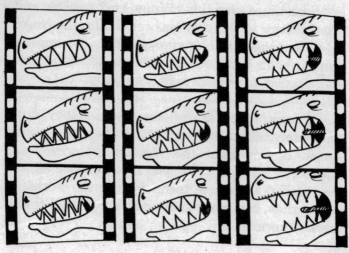

If you show those pictures on a movie projector, the creature will look as if it's alive and opening its mouth. Add a suitable sound effect, plus some shots of tiny people in post-production and suddenly you'll see a huge, roaring monster on the screen.

Unfortunately stop-motion has one big problem – the pictures are too good. If you film someone walking, their movement will make each individual frame slightly blurred and that blurring makes the movement look very natural when viewed on screen.

With stop-motion, the monster is absolutely still when each individual picture is shot. That means each frame is crystal clear and the lack of blurring makes the movement look slightly jerky on screen. This doesn't matter on animated films like *Chicken Run*, as you've nothing to compare it with but, if you combine live action with this kind of animation in a normal movie, it never looks completely realistic.

Despite this problem, stop-motion was used extensively in the past because there was no alternative. It brought King Kong to life, made mythical creatures attack Jason and the Argonauts and sent the snow walkers striding across the landscape in *The Empire Strikes Back*. But it wasn't just used for monsters. It also animated puppet stand-ins for actors in dangerous situations like the runaway mine cart in *Indiana Jones and the Temple of Doom* and, as long ago as 1937, it made a pen appear to write by itself in *Topper*.

But now there is no need to mix stop-motion with live action. Computer technology has improved so much that it's possible to create realistic digital monsters which only exist on screen.

Computer magic

The arrival of computers transformed the movie effects business. Digital drawing tools replaced brushes and paint for producing matte paintings and made it possible to paint wires out of a shot and replace an overcast sky with a clear one.

Once movie makers started using computers, it was a natural progression to move from creating settings to trying to create characters as well. The very first computer-drawn character appeared in a movie called *Young Sherlock Holmes* (1985) when a knight in a stained-glass window came to life. It was lucky he was supposed to be flat and unrealistic, for the computer tools available then were much more limited than they are now.

The next stage in computer-generated characters was aliens like the T1000 in *Terminator 2*. This robot from the future was supposedly made of liquid metal which could assume any shape. Much of the time, its chosen shape was a policeman played by actor Robert Patrick, but when it changed from one shape into another, computer-generated images took over. To help create the liquid metal version of the policeman, the effects team painted a black grid on the actor to help scan his shape and way of moving into the computer.

WHEN YOU SAID YOU'D PAINT ME, I WAS EXPECTING A PORTRAIT

Creating aliens was easy compared to the challenges of producing digital images that looked like creatures we're more familiar with. The breakthrough came in 1993 with *Jurassic Park*, but initially even the producer, Steven Spielberg, thought it would only be possible to use computer-generated images for distant herd scenes. He planned to use traditional stop-motion for the other dinosaur scenes with that all important blurring added by computer.

But the effects team at Industrial Light and Magic were sure they could do better than this. They produced some sample dinosaur footage which impressed Spielberg so much that he abandoned all his plans for stop-motion and used computer-generated dinosaurs instead. The resulting movie stunned audiences around the world and proved that computers could make monsters.

Now computer-generated images are used in many movies and adverts and they are not just dinosaurs. Lions, gorillas and a host of other animals find their way on screen via computer wizardry and digital people add bulk to crowd scenes and passengers to cruise liners.

Creating computer creatures

The creation of an on-screen creature often starts with a clay model which is scanned into the computer. Then the effects team have to work out how it might move, what colour it will be and how the light will reflect from its coat. If they are copying a real animal, these decisions are based on looking at the real thing, but they can use their imagination more freely with aliens and monsters.

To make the audience believe the digital creature is really there, it must affect its surroundings. So if you want to add a digital giant hamster to a scene in your film, you must make sure that it makes splashes in the water as it wades through a pond, moves the branches it brushes against and breaks the rays of light it walks through. It's also important that the actors react as if it's really there.

The light ray problems can be solved on screen in post-production. The other environmental effects need to be dealt with when you are filming and this usually involves men with sticks or, in the case of ponds, large rubber boots.

- To make your hamster splash in a river, film someone in boots jumping in the water. Then replace him with the hamster in post-production.

AARGH! IT'S HORRIFIC!

SPLASH!

98

- To make your hamster move branches, film someone with a big stick running along the creature's path hitting the branches. Then replace both him and his stick with the digital hamster in post-production.

- To make your hamster collapse a shelf by knocking against it, first build a collapsible shelf like the one on page 76. Film it collapsing, then add the hamster in post-production.
- To make sure everyone looks at the right place when they scream in terror, have someone with a big stick stand where the hamster will be. This works even better if you have a mark or a couple of tennis balls on the stick to show where the monster's eyes will be. Then everyone in the shot will be looking at its eyes just as they would in real life.

If you want the actors to do more with the hamster than just look at it or run away, they will need more than a man with a stick to help them. They need something real to act with – something they can touch and which will move in the right way.

In *The Phantom Menace*, it was vital that the actors and the surroundings reacted properly to Jar Jar, a computer-generated alien who actually had to act. To make his scenes convincing, another actor stood in for him during the filming. He wasn't as tall as Jar Jar so he had a model of the alien's head on top of his own and his own eyes were covered by a dark visor to encourage the actors to look at Jar Jar's eyes instead of his. When the filming was over, the actor was replaced by the computer-generated Jar Jar in post-production.

Often the actors don't need to have the whole monster on set. For many scenes, all they need is a face, a foot or a tail which looks like part of the monster and moves realistically. Making this type of prop is a job for the puppeteers and animatronics experts. Both *Jurassic Park* and the TV series *Walking with Dinosaurs* used animatronics for this type of close-up work.

AMAZING ANIMATRONICS

Animatronics is about puppets and a puppet at its simplest is a sock. A skilled puppeteer can put his hand in the sock and make it come alive. If you add arms to the sock and attach them to rods, the puppeteer can move those with his other hand, bringing new realism to your sock monster. Some eyes, some hair and a mouth add more character and before you know it, you have a Muppet.

HOLDING A PUPPET UP LIKE THIS FOR A LONG TIME MAKES YOUR ARMS ACHE...

IF YOU'RE GOING TO DO IT, TRY DOING SOME EXERCISES IN ADVANCE TO BUILD UP YOUR MUSCLES

GYM

PHYSICAL

Of course, there's nothing very scary about a sock. If you want to create a believable alien monster, you need lips that curl into a snarl, nostrils that flare and eyes that follow its prey around the room. There is no way just a hand inside a glove puppet can produce all these movements. If you want

to animate a puppet as skilfully as this, you need some mechanical wizardry to help you, and it is this technology which is called animatronics.

Building the puppet

An animatronic creature starts as sketches on paper and maybe a small clay model, but the actual manufacturing process begins with a full-size clay model. When that is finished, it's used to make a fibreglass or plaster mould and that mould in turn is used to make the outer skin of the creature from latex, foam latex or silicone.

That skin has to hold all the mechanisms which will make the creature move. The smaller the creature, the harder it is to fit everything inside, so sometimes several versions are made, each designed to perform different movements. For instance, for an alien the size of a cat, the head may only contain enough space for a few movements – maybe eyes side to side, eyes up and down, eyes close and mouth open.

The mechanisms for those movements may look something like this:

I'M NOT FEELING QUITE MYSELF TODAY

That's good enough for distance shots, but it won't look completely realistic in close-ups. For those, it's worth making a much larger head with room inside for all the sophisticated lip, tongue and face muscle movements you need to make it look really alive. It will still look the same size as the other puppet on screen so no one will spot the trick.

ATTACK FROM PLANET HAMSTER

ORDER FORM

URGENT

To the animatronics workshop
Please supply:
Six very small non-animated hamsters to be sucked up into mother ship.
Three small hamsters with moving heads for model shots.
One giant hamster head for close-ups with full facial expressions and a mouth large enough to pick up Gloria.
One fully animated hamster paw to crash through lorry roof.
One hamster bottom large enough to crush Gloria's boss by sitting on him, but light enough to not really hurt him.

Making it work

However good the puppet, making it look real depends on the skill of the puppeteers who make it move. As they only have two hands, it sometimes takes several of them working at once to operate a complicated puppet – a situation which can take lots of rehearsal to get right. It's particularly hard to coordinate several people operating different parts of a creature's face, so sometimes the movements are pre-programmed into a computer. This allows one puppeteer to make it smile or snarl without having to individually control the many different movements which make up that expression.

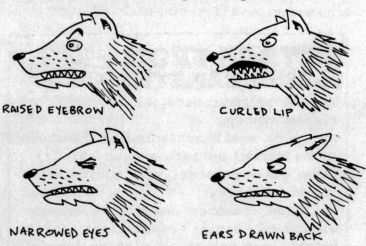

RAISED EYEBROW

CURLED LIP

NARROWED EYES

EARS DRAWN BACK

Hiding the puppeteers isn't a problem with movies, as both they and the controls can be taken out in post-production if necessary. To help with this process, the puppeteers dress in blue if they are working in front of a blue screen or another colour which is easy to isolate if they are on an ordinary set.

The puppeteers need to be hidden for a live performance so puppets on stage often appear on tables or over the backs of settees. Radio control works well as the puppeteer can hide in the wings, and cables are good too, provided no one trips over them.

The skeletal C-3PO in *The Phantom Menace* was worked by a puppeteer standing behind him. He wore a helmet with rods attached to the puppet's head so whenever he moved his head, C-3PO's head moved too. Other rods attached his legs to the puppet's legs so when he walked, C-3PO walked too. It was impossible for him to hide so he had to be taken out in post-production. To do this, the computer effects team used a picture of the set without C-3PO and the puppeteer. From this "clean plate", they took pieces of the picture to fill in the spaces left when they removed the puppeteer from each frame.

Never work with animals

Using animals on stage and screen can cause all sorts of problems. They are hard to direct, bite the actors and make puddles (or worse) on the floor. Even highly-trained ones have their limitations – you can't ask them to do things which are too difficult or dangerous. That's when film directors turn to animatronic stand-ins for the real thing.

Suppose you're putting on a play which needs two live ducks in a crate during one of the scenes. If you use real ducks, you will need someone to look after them and they may start quacking at an inconvenient moment. If you use model ducks they won't look real because they don't move. But if you use animatronics inside the models to make them move their heads from time to time, the audience will happily accept that they are alive.

106

Performing dogs and talking pigs

Animatronic puppies played a vital part in the live action movie of *101 Dalmatians* where they took the place of the real puppies for dangerous or difficult scenes. The stand-ins made by Jim Henson's Creature Shop had silicon skin painted with a pattern of spots to match the puppies they were replacing.

That movie didn't just use animatronic puppies. One scene involved the real puppies suckling from a friendly cow, but they weren't allowed near a real cow in case they caught a disease. The solution was an animatronic cow with an udder that really supplied milk. The Creature Shop only made the rear half of it as that was all that was seen in the suckling shot. A real cow was used for the other shots.

Another movie that used both animatronic animals and real ones was *Babe*. This tale about a pig who learnt to be a sheep dog would have been impossible to make without its incredible special effects. Computer graphics made the real animals look as if they were talking and stunningly lifelike animatronics took over when the demands of the plot were too hard for the trained animals.

Fishy facts

The most famous fishy film ever made was *Jaws*. Sharks are unpredictable and dangerous so animatronic sharks were used in many of the shots. Three of them were made – one which could be towed behind a boat for front views and two other full-length sharks for side views. Both of these were really only half a shark – one right-hand side and one left-hand one (no *Titanic*-style flopping here!).

107

To add authenticity, the animatronic sharks were replaced with shots of real sharks wherever possible. One important real shot involved a man going shark-hunting underwater in a metal cage.

Unfortunately, the only real shark which took any interest in him was considerably smaller than the 7.5-metre star of the film. But the effects team didn't give up. Instead they sent down a very short person in a smaller cage which made the real shark look much bigger.

Ordinary fish are far less exciting than man-eating ones, but they still feature sometimes in films. In *Perfect Storm*, the fishing boat had to be able to haul in a catch of live swordfish – an impossible task when the boat is in an indoor tank. Once again animatronics solved the problem by creating amazingly lifelike fish which thrashed about convincingly on the deck.

Puppet problems

Animatronic puppets have to cope with plenty of wear and tear. They often have to perform the same action over and over again or put up with rough treatment in an action film. Even if they are sturdily built, they often need repairs between takes. The sharks in *Jaws* needed a regular supply of teeth to replace the lost and broken ones (rubber for biting people, hard for biting objects).

In one production of the stage play *Blue Remembered Hills*, the production team needed a squirrel to fall out of a tree and wriggle on the ground as if injured. They already had a lifelike fur fabric squirrel so they only needed to add the wriggle. To do this, they bought a crawling Action Man, cut it in half and put the bottom end in their puppet.

GET READY FOR ... ACTION SQUIRREL!

This worked beautifully on test. The problem came when they dropped the squirrel out of the tree for the first time. It hit the ground with a thud and lay motionless – the impact had smashed the Action Man mechanism. They had forgotten to build in durability.

At this point, they called in an animatronics expert. He replaced the Action Man with a much stronger radio-controlled mechanism which he wrapped in foam before putting it in the squirrel. The production team provided extra protection in the form of a soft mat for the squirrel to land on and the end result was a durable effect which worked for the whole run of the play.

DEVASTATING DISASTERS

Disasters are dramatic. They are exciting to watch, add nail-biting tension and give heroes a wonderful excuse to be heroic. No wonder audiences and script-writers love them.

Producing a disaster to order is a real challenge for the special effects team. They have to make it look as dramatic and dangerous as possible while minimising the real damage and keeping everyone safe. So, if you want to add fires, explosions and car chases to *Attack from Planet Hamster*, don't try to do them yourself. Let Eric do them instead. He's an expert at this type of effect and has the all-important pyrotechnics certificate to allow him to use explosives.

Fire! Fire!

Fire adds drama to explosions, provides burning buildings for daring rescues and, when safely confined to a fireplace, adds cosiness to indoor scenes. But fire has to be used with extreme care. If it gets out of hand, it can easily cause a real disaster.

One of the most famous fire disaster movies ever made was *Towering Inferno*. The story is about a fire destroying a skyscraper 138 storeys high and the desperate attempts to rescue the people trapped inside. Safety was a high priority for the production team so they had the Los Angeles Fire Department present all the time. No individual fire was allowed to burn for more than 30 seconds – the effect of a long, continuous fire was produced by joining many short scenes together. It's a credit to the effects team that, despite the number of fires, falls and cascades of water involved in the movie, the only casualty was a fire officer who cut his hand on some broken glass.

Live action blazes

Fire is particularly difficult on stage. The risk of burning down the theatre is so great that you can't use the real thing. Fortunately most people believe the old saying "There's no smoke without fire", so you can make them think the set is alight by putting in plenty of smoke combined with flickering yellow and orange lighting. If you must show some flames, strips of very light orange or yellow silk blown by a fan can look surprisingly effective in the smoke.

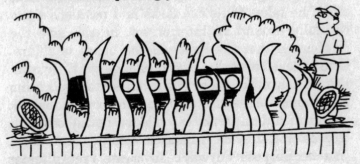

Real flames and raging infernos

Despite the effectiveness of smoke and lighting effects, there comes a time in many movies when they just aren't enough and you need to add real flames. That's the point at which Eric gets out the flame forks – long pipes with several jets at the end which, when connected to a gas supply, burn with an easily controlled, reasonably safe flame, rather like a large version of the ones you get on bunsen burners at school.

With a few flame forks in the windows of a house, plus plenty of smoke, he can give the impression that the house is burning without damaging it at all. If he takes the same forks and positions them carefully around an interior set, he can give the impression that the inside of the house is ablaze. Often these effects look good enough on their own, but he can make them look even better by adding extra computer-generated flames in post-production.

Although flame forks can make a house look as if it is on fire, they can't make it actually burn down (not on purpose anyway). To create raging forest fires, blazing tower blocks and roofs collapsing in flames, Eric makes models and sets them alight.

Unfortunately, small flames don't look quite the same as full-size ones so, to make them look more convincing, he films them with a high-speed camera. When this is shown at the standard 24 frames per second, the action is slowed down, which helps hide the fact that it is a model.

When David Selznick filmed the burning of Atlanta for *Gone with the Wind*, he was so keen to make it look realistic that he wouldn't use a model shot. Instead he set fire to the whole of the outside set at the studio plus several other disused sets which were close to it. The resulting blaze was entirely convincing on screen and took thousands of gallons of water to put out.

Hot camera tricks

For safety, the actors and the flames need to be as far apart as possible. But to make the danger seem real, they need to look as if they are very close to each other. The solution to this dilemma lies in clever photography.

Long focus lenses are designed for photographing things a long way away. Nature photographers use them to take close-ups of wildlife from a distance.

This kind of lens makes it look as if the distance from the camera to the animal is much shorter than it really is and this foreshortening effect is very useful in filming fires. The actor can stand a safe distance from the flames but look as if he's really close to them.

ACTING!

Explosions

OUTSIDE THE HAMSTERS' HEADQUARTERS -
DAY
Hans and Gloria rush out of the front
door, anxious to get away before the
extermination unit self-destructs. But
the hamsters have posted guards on the
opposite roof who spot their escape. One
fires an anti-tank gun at them but (as
he is a villain) he misses and blows up
a nearby phone box instead.

One of the problems with explosions is the flying
debris they produce. Blowing up a real phone box
would send shards of glass and metal flying through
the air that could seriously injure cameramen,
directors and unsuspecting spectators. So, to
minimize the danger, Eric uses a replica phone box
made of lightweight materials joined together with
such weak joints that it will break apart easily.
Then he only needs a very small amount of
explosive to blow it apart and the debris is light
pieces of plastic, foam or polystyrene which won't
hurt anyone.

Hans and Gloria flee across the gravel
car park. The guard fires another round
which slams into the ground a short
distance from Hans, sending a plume of
earth and stones into the air and knocking
a passer-by off her feet.

One option for this shot would be to bury a mortar in the ground packed with a small amount of explosive plus small pieces of cork and polystyrene. These will fly up easily into the air and look like earth and pebbles. But for this scene, Eric decides to use a safer device called a whoofer. This is packed with cork and polystyrene and buried in the ground just like the mortar, but instead of containing explosive, it's worked by a surge of compressed air.

RAT-TAT-TAT-TAT!!

Of course, there's no bang – just a whoof of air (hence the name) – so you'll have to add a bright flash and the sound of an explosion in post-production.

The passer-by is a stunt woman wearing padding under her clothes to protect her when she lands. She could just fall over but that wouldn't look as dramatic as if she was blown into the air. To make this happen, Eric stands her on a gadget called an air ram which uses compressed air to shoot her into the air at exactly the right time. He could have asked her to wear a jerk harness attached to a wire instead and pulled her off her feet as the whoofer went off.

I DON'T USUALLY GET SUCH A GOOD REACTION

WHOOF!

> Another guard starts shooting at Hans and Gloria with a machine-gun. The bullets spatter into the ground around their feet as they run for their lives.

The traditional way of doing this effect is to bury small explosive charges called squibs in the ground. Their position is carefully marked so the actors can avoid treading on them and they are detonated one after the other by remote control. However, Eric decides on the newer, safer option of adding digital bullet hits in post-production.

> Suddenly the exterminator self-destructs and the hamster headquarters is blown apart.

All the location shots have used the local high school as the hamster headquarters but, despite encouragement from some of the students, it's impossible for Eric to blow up the real building. So to produce this important effect, Eric builds a model. The larger it is, the better the explosion will look, so this one is two metres tall and made of lightweight materials that will blow apart easily. He rigs the model with small quantities of explosive positioned to produce the maximum effect for the cameras.

To make the scene even more spectacular, he carefully places plastic containers of highly flammable fuel inside. When he blows up the model, the explosives set fire to the fuel to produce billowing balls of flame. As this type of flame moves extremely fast, he maximises the dramatic effect by filming it at high speed to slow down the action on screen.

Hans and Gloria leap into their car and roar away at high speed, hotly pursued by the hamsters' guards in another car.

When you watch a movie, this kind of car chase looks like one continuous sequence but it isn't. It's made up of several different stunts, each filmed separately with breaks in between to set up new situations and, if necessary, to repair the cars.

In order to film a car chase you need a road, and that takes advance organization. To avoid getting your actors stuck in a traffic jam, you could:

- Film early in the morning (with police permission).
- Arrange for some roads to be closed for you to film in.
- Film on a newly-built road that hasn't been opened yet.
- Film on an old airfield using the runway as a road.
- Film on an outside set at the studio.

> Hans and Gloria speed along a road, only to find to their horror that it ends at the canal. They can't turn back - their pursuers are too close behind - so Hans puts his foot on the accelerator and hurtles towards the canal bank. The car jumps the gap and lands safely the other side.

To make a car take off like this, you need to drive it up a ramp in much the same way as you would to jump on a skateboard or a BMX bike. Eric doesn't want the audience to see the ramp, so he hides it behind a conveniently parked lorry. For the jump, Hans and Gloria are replaced by two stuntmen and their car is replaced by an identical one with a reinforced internal cage and the bare minimum of petrol in the tank.

How did they do that?

There's often more than one way to create a special effect. How do you think these tricky scenes were created?

1. In *Poltergeist*, a house implodes, collapsing in on itself and disappearing into a black hole at its centre. How did the movie makers produce this effect?

a) They built an inflatable house, pulled out the stopper and filmed it deflating.

b) They built a miniature house which they pulled into a funnel using a combination of wires and a strong vacuum.

c) They used a real house rigged with cables attached to a fast moving lorry.

2. Silent comedian Harold Lloyd was famous for the movie scenes where he perched on the edges of roofs, dangled from windowsills or balanced on high ledges. To film these, did he...

a) perform the routines high up on real buildings?
b) use a stunt double?
c) use specially-built studio sets so he was really only a metre above the ground?

3. In *Terminator 2: Judgement Day*, the Terminator, played by Arnold Schwarzenegger, had to have a metal pipe pushed through his body. Did the effects team...

a) use a trick pipe that collapsed into itself as it was put into Arnie with the other end added in post-production?
b) use a trick pipe which went into the front of Arnie's costume, curved round his side under his shirt and then came out at the back?
c) use a full-size Terminator puppet so the pipe could really go through it?

4. In *The X-Files Movie*, a bee had to walk across Scully's collar. Did the effects team...

a) use a radio-controlled model of a bee?
b) add a computer-generated bee in post-production?

c) use a real bee that followed a scent trail across Scully's collar?

5. When a small town was terrified by a horde of particularly nasty, small creatures in *Gremlins*, the movie makers brought the invaders to life on screen using...
a) radio-controlled puppets.
b) glove puppets.
c) string puppets.

6. There had to be several retakes of the scene in *Close Encounters of the Third Kind*, where the aliens come out of the spaceship. What kept going wrong?
a) The aliens were played by puppets whose strings kept tangling.
b) The aliens were played by six-year-old girls who kept disco dancing.
c) The aliens were played by chimpanzees who kept fighting.

7. In *ET*, Elliot cycles into the sky with the friendly alien in his bicycle basket. To film this famous shot, did the effects team use...
a) a bicycle with a helicopter rotor blade that was painted out in post-production?
b) the actor playing Elliot riding a real bicycle suspended on wires?
c) a model bicycle ridden by a puppet Elliot?

8. *Jumanji* features a stampede of many different animals including elephants, zebras and rhinoceroses. How did the effects team create this scene?

a) They used computer-generated animals.

b) They filmed many different animals one at a time and then combined all the shots into one scene during post-production.

c) They hired a selection of animals from San Francisco Zoo and encouraged them to chase a lorry loaded with food.

9. In *Death Becomes Her*, Meryl Streep twists her head right round so she can look behind her. To film this, did the director...

a) combine a shot of her head looking one way with a shot of her body looking the other way and add a computer-generated twist in her neck?

b) make Meryl Streep train for two months with a contortionist so she could perform the trick herself?

c) use a puppet replica of Meryl Streep with a revolving head?

10. The *Dr Who* TV series was famous for its chases down endless corridors or tunnels. Were these created...

a) by matting blue-screen shots of the actors on to a miniature maze guaranteed to fool even the most intelligent of rats?

b) by filming on location in the endless corridors of

Broadcasting House which were suitably decorated for the occasion?

c) by building a set of a small piece of corridor and filming the actors running down it over and over again?

Answers:

1. b) This ambitious effect was particularly difficult as there was only one chance to get it right. It was filmed with a very high speed camera to slow down the implosion on screen.

2. a) Harold Lloyd always performed his stunts himself and he was always as high above the ground as it appeared on screen.

3. c) The puppet was designed to move just like Arnie and it needed a whole team of puppeteers to operate it.

4. c) The bee was such a natural performer that it repeated its walk perfectly for each take.

5. All of them plus cable-controlled puppets. Different types of puppet were used to fit in with the needs of different scenes.

6. b) Little girls were used to make the aliens much smaller than humans but they were hard to direct because they were so young.

7. c) A motor turned the bicycle wheels which, in turn, turned the pedals to make the puppet look as if he was pedalling. The shot of the puppet on the bike was combined with a background shot of the moon to make the final scene.

8. a) Filming all these different animals close together would have been nightmarishly difficult, so computer-generated images were used instead. It was the first time they'd been used for furry animals and the lion's mane was particularly tricky to create. Although **b)** wasn't used for *Jumanji*, it was used successfully in the 1929 movie, *Noah's Ark*.

9. a) Before the development of computer graphics, this effect would probably have been done with a puppet.

10. c) The budget for *Dr Who* wasn't large enough to build complicated sets so the programme makers had to make the most of what they had. They changed camera angles and moved features like rocks and doorways between shots to give the impression the actors were in a different place.

BUCKETS OF BLOOD AND OTHER GORY BITS

Action movies, murder mysteries and hospital dramas all have one thing in common – lots of blood. You can buy fake blood for use in this sort of effect or, with a bit of experiment in the kitchen, you can make your own. Start by making a liquid of the right consistency and then colour it.

Design your own blood

Blood is thicker than water but you may want to vary the consistency a bit for different effects. To make large quantities pour out of a dead body and make a pool on the floor, you'll want it quite runny. To dab on fake wounds so they look like bloody flesh, you'll want it sticky so it doesn't trickle off.

Golden syrup makes good sticky blood. It tends to attract insects, but so does the real thing so this may add authenticity as well as being a nuisance. You can make it runnier by adding small quantities of washing-up liquid and/or water.

An alternative starting-point for runny blood is cornflour or arrowroot, mixed with water and boiled until it thickens. You can use instant gravy powder if you prefer, but this works out expensive for large quantities. Be careful not to burn yourself or your actors – let it cool right down before you use it.

Colouring blood

To colour your fake blood, add red food colouring or non-toxic red powder paint. This gives a bright red colour, so you may want to darken it by adding a little brown – a few drops of very strong black coffee works well. Of course, if you've used gravy powder as your starting-point, the brown is already there so you will automatically get a dark red.

> Fake blood can stain clothes. If you have to put it on a costume you want to use again, wash it out before the blood dries. If you can't wash the blood out, you'll need to have some spare costumes available.

Taking the easy way out

If you don't want to buy fake blood and you don't want to make it yourself, you can always try using tomato ketchup, strawberry sauce or jam. If you are filming in black and white, the blood will look more authentic if it's black or dark brown rather than red, so you can try using chocolate syrup. That's what Alfred Hitchcock used when his heroine was stabbed in the shower in *Psycho*.

Making people bleed

Providing the blood is only part of the challenge. For a really gruesome effect, you have to make it look as if it's coming out of someone. This is easiest with injuries which are supposed to have already happened as you can create them out of sight of the audience.

To create a cut or bullet wound, first make a clay model of the injury you want. Then use the model to create a mould and the mould to produce a thin latex copy of your wound.

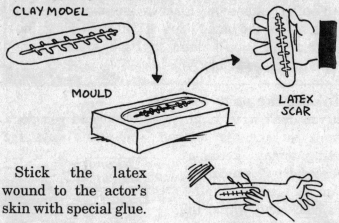

CLAY MODEL

MOULD

LATEX SCAR

Stick the latex wound to the actor's skin with special glue.

Use make-up and fake blood to disguise the edges of the latex and make the wound look realistic.

When the scene is over, just peel off the latex and your actor is healed.

IT'S A MIRACLE!

Injuries that happen in front of the audience are more difficult, but there's a number of tricks you can use to make them look real. To help you understand these, Eric and Presto have got together to produce:

THE MAGICAL GUIDE TO BLOODY EFFECTS

The blood-soaked sponge trick

You must have seen a scene like this hundreds of times.

In reality, the actor has a blood-soaked sponge stored safely under his shirt in a plastic bag. The bag has some holes at the top so, when he presses it with his hands, the blood squirts out of the sponge on to his shirt.

Alternatively, the blood can be in a container which will burst under the pressure of his hands.

That way you don't need a sponge and the effect will be more immediate but there is always the risk that the container won't break when required.

The disappearing blade trick

There are two kinds of trick knife. The first type has a safe plastic or wooden blade which sinks back into the handle when it's pressed. This allows the murderer to plunge the knife into his victim's back with the blade disappearing convincingly from view. This combines well with the blood-soaked sponge trick – the knife presses on the sponge to produce a realistic patch of blood.

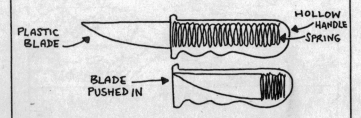

PLASTIC BLADE

HOLLOW HANDLE

SPRING

BLADE PUSHED IN

The blood-filled knife trick

The other type of trick knife has the blood in the handle with a very thin tube running down the blade to the tip. As the murderer cuts his victim's throat, he presses the handle of the knife which sends a stream of blood down the tube. With practice, he can leave a realistic line of blood on his victim's throat.

I THINK YOU NEED MORE PRACTICE

The growing pool of blood trick

The victim falls to the floor fatally wounded, but she makes sure she lands on a prearranged spot where a small tube comes through a hole in the stage. Attached to that tube is a pump with a good supply of fairly runny blood. The pump sends a stream of it through the hole which spreads out convincingly so the victim looks as if she's lying in a growing pool of blood.

IT'LL BE MURDER TRYING TO CLEAN THIS FLOOR

The blood squirting from wound trick

This is a variation on the pool of blood trick which is useful for severed arteries and bullet wounds. Instead of having the tube through the floor, attach it to the actor so the open end is at the point of the wound. Then pump the blood out at the required moment.

Gruesome body scenes

Some scenes don't just need the actor to bleed – they need him to have his chest ripped open or his leg cut off. As even very dedicated actors aren't willing to sacrifice their body parts in the cause of art, this is another job for the effects team.

The solution to the problem is to cleverly combine fake bits of body with the real one and the easiest way to do this is with holes cut in the floor or table. So to show someone having their leg cut off without anaesthetic, you can lie the actor on a table so one leg goes down through a hole by her knee where it is hidden by the sheet over the table. Put a fake leg where her lower leg would have been and arrange another sheet to cover the join.

THIS MAY STING A LITTLE

FAKE LEG
(JOINT
COVERED)

REAL LEG HIDDEN

Now the surgeon can operate on the fake leg while the patient writhes around in agony and screams.

FX challenge

Suppose you want to film a scene where an alien that has been growing inside a human suddenly bursts out of its host's chest. This is hardly an original idea – *Alien* did it with such dramatic effect that it's now become a popular concept in sci-fi films. So how would you do it?

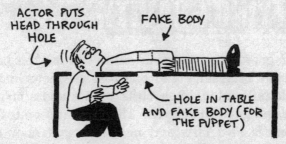

ACTOR PUTS HEAD THROUGH HOLE

FAKE BODY

HOLE IN TABLE AND FAKE BODY (FOR THE PUPPET)

One solution is to make a fake body with no head. Lie it on a table and get the actor to crouch underneath with his head through a hole so it looks as if it's attached to the body. Now put a puppeteer under the table too, with a glove puppet alien which he can put through another hole in the table and push out through the fake chest at the required moment.

OK, Mr Clever Dick Illustrator, this is not a foolproof solution. It demands excellent coordination between the puppeteer and the actor and a realistic alien long enough to cover the puppeteer's arm.

Other ways to make it even more realistic are:

- Cover the alien in sticky goo.
- Make lots of blood and bits of raw meat pop out at the same time.

Maybe you can think of an even better method.

DEFYING GRAVITY

What goes up, must come down. That's the basic principle of gravity and one reason why so many people fall off buildings, cliffs, planes and a myriad other things in the movies. The other reason is that audiences love falls and near misses – they add drama to action films and slapstick humour to comedies.

In real life, falls can be a painful experience. Even the proverbial slip on a banana skin can result in a bruised backside, and tumbling from a plane puts your life severely at risk. So falls and near misses are another part of movie making that needs the special effects team.

The illusion of height

Hans and Gloria are locked in an empty office while the giant hamsters continue their plan to take over the world. There is no way out except the window but the office is on the thirtieth floor. Bravely, Hans and Gloria climb out and start to inch their way along a ledge. Suddenly Gloria slips and falls but Hans catches her wrist and stops her. She dangles from his grasp as he, slowly and painfully, pulls her back to safety.

The first step in filming this is to persuade the audience that Hans and Gloria really are high above the ground. Make Hans walk to the window and look out. Then cut to an establishing shot of a view from a really high window.

For the next section, you need a set which is a replica of part of the outside of the building. It needs to include the window and the section of ledge, but you don't need the rest of the building. That can be added later in post-production.

The ledge only needs to be high enough to let Gloria dangle from it. The audience won't see that her feet are only half a metre from the floor. Neither will they see the mattresses covering the floor to protect anyone who really falls off.

You are now ready to start filming as Hans and Gloria climb out. You'll add to the illusion of height if you position one of the cameras below them looking up – ask the cameraman to lie on the floor if necessary. Occasionally make one of the actors look down again so you can cut in another establishing shot of how far down it is to the ground.

Tumbling from tall places

Pretend high places work well for near misses but run into problems if you need someone to really fall off.

Hans and Gloria are on the roof when the leader of the hamster's human henchmen spots them. He rushes towards them with a knife raised to attack, but Hans springs out of the way. Unable to stop himself, the attacker hurtles past him and over the edge, falling to his death on the roof of a car far below.

There are several ways to tackle this depending on the budget you have available.

Method 1 – let's pretend

This makes the audience's imagination do all the work.

1. Film the attack on the roof – you can use a real flat roof or a set.

2. Film the henchman rushing towards the edge.

3. Now film a shot looking down at the henchman lying on the crumpled roof of a car. It's good if you can film this from high up and then zoom down on to the detail of the body. Add a bit of blood for added drama.

4. Now put the shots together in sequence and the audience will assume he fell, even though they didn't see it.

Method 2 – Stunts R Us

This uses the same sequence as Method 1 with a couple of extra shots. To film it you need a stunt man who is good at falls and roughly the same size as the actor playing the attacker. Disguise him so the two of them look the same from a distance. Then film him rushing across the roof and over the edge. Another camera can film him actually falling, waving his arms and legs dramatically to prove he's not a dummy, before he lands safely on a large air bag. Of course, the audience won't see him land – you'll cut to the shot of the body on the car instead.

Method 3 – dummies don't die

Again, this uses the same sequence as Method 1 with one extra shot between the rush across the roof and the landing. You don't need a stunt man this time – just a dummy dressed to look like the attacker that you can throw off the roof after making sure it won't land on anyone walking past.

You can film this fall all the way down to the ground, but the audience may spot it's a dummy because it isn't moving.

Method 4 – virtual reality

Instead of using a dummy or a stunt man, you can use a computer to create a shot of the man falling. It will work best if you scan in the details of the actor first so the digital stunt man looks and moves as much like him as possible. As with all computer-generated images, its success will depend on both the quality of the software and the skill of the operator.

Plunging from planes

Suppose the producer decides the scene on the roof isn't exciting enough so he moves it to a plane.

> Hans and Gloria are on the ~~roof~~ *A PLANE* when the leader of the hamster's human henchmen spots them. He rushes towards them with a knife raised to attack, but Hans springs out of the way. Unable to stop himself, the attacker hurtles past him and ~~over the~~ *OUT OF THE PLANE DOOR* edge, falling to his death on ~~the roof of a car~~ far below.

To make this look really dramatic, you can use a stunt man – one who's good at free-fall parachute jumping. He dresses up as the attacker in a costume cleverly designed so it's loose enough to hide a parachute underneath the top. When he falls out, he looks as if he's falling to his death but, after the

138

cameras have stopped filming, he opens the hidden parachute and lands safely.

Disappearing down black holes

If you want someone falling into oblivion, you can use a camera trick to help you. Lie your actor on the floor which you have already covered with some blue-screen material.

Now ask him to wave his arms and legs in a suitable fashion while you film him with a zoom lens. Start with the lens in its long focus position so he looks very big and zoom out rapidly so he seems to get smaller and smaller. In post-production, you can add this image to a background of space, a blazing inferno or a swirling vortex and you'll have the shot you want.

You can try this at home if you have a video camera with a zoom lens. As you can't easily do the post-production stage, film your actor lying on a black floor so he looks as if he's falling into a black hole.

Leaping from lorries

Hans makes his escape in a lorry, not knowing that the hamsters have gnawed through the brake pipe. Unable to stop the speeding vehicle, he jumps out just moments before it crashes into a wall.

Although this scene must end up looking as if it all happened at once, you can film it in sections.

1. An establishing shot of the speeding lorry.

2. A shot of Hans in the cab pushing the door open.

3. A close-up of him jumping out.

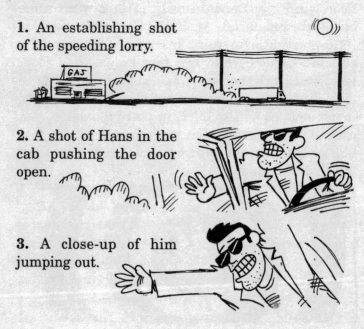

4. A shot of him rolling on the ground.

5. A shot of the lorry crashing, which could be a model shot to save the lorry.

At first glance, the jumping and landing shots look like a job for a stunt double, but that won't work here. The director is keen to have a close-up, so Hans must do it himself.

The solution is to use another bit of trick photography. When you look out of the window of a moving car, it looks as if you are still and the trees and houses are moving. In the same way, if you film with a moving camera, the resulting pictures look as if the camera was standing still and the things you were filming were moving.

So put Hans in the lorry while it is standing still in front of a blue screen. Then film him jumping out safely on to a mattress with a camera that's moving quickly past him. When you look at the shot, it will look as if the lorry is moving. In the final scene you'll cut away from this shot before he hits the mattress and put in a shot of Hans rolling over on the ground as if he has just landed from the jump.

YOU CAN USE THIS MOVING-CAMERA TECHNIQUE TO MAKE MODEL SPACESHIPS LOOK AS IF THEY ARE MOVING THROUGH SPACE. ALWAYS MOVE THE CAMERA IN THE OPPOSITE DIRECTION FROM THE ONE YOU WANT THE SHIPS TO GO

Superheroes and fairies

In fantasy, anything is possible – for instance, people can fly. In real life, flying sequences on stage and screen need special effects to make them work. There is nothing new about this kind of effect. The ancient Greeks were doing it 2,500 years ago with a hand-operated crane which lifted actors playing the gods down from heaven and carried them away again. It wasn't just used for gods – one Greek play needs a philosopher carried in a flying basket and another requires a flying chariot.

Today the most important equipment for creating flying effects is the flying harness worn by the actor. This fits tightly round his hips and the top of his legs. Unless the harness itself is part of the plot (as it was in *Mission Impossible*), it's worn under the costume so the audience can't see it.

NO, NO. IT'S JUST YOUR UNDERPANTS YOU WEAR OVER YOUR TIGHTS

There is a thin wire attached to each side of the harness and these in turn are attached to the flying rig above the stage or set. This has a pulley system which allows a technician off-stage to control the actor's height above the ground. This kind of harness isn't just used to make people look as if they are flying. You can also use it for those spectacular leaps in Kung Fu style fight scenes and to make people look as if they are weightless in outer space.

The wires are very thin so they are hard to see, especially on stage where the actors are a long way from the audience. If they do show up when you're filming a movie, you can take them out in post-production.

If you film an actor flying in front of a blue screen, you can then combine his image with any background you like in post-production. So, for *Superman*, you'd add the sky, and for Tinkerbell you'd add a background close-up of Peter Pan's face just as the effects team did in *Hook*. By doing this, they made her look tiny and she looked even more like a fairy when they used a computer to attach some flapping wings they had filmed separately.

Human flies

Another way to defy gravity is by walking up walls and along ceilings. This is almost impossible to do on stage, but crops up sometimes in movies, especially ones about space travel or superheroes.

Of course, the only place anyone can really walk is on the ground so the secret behind this type of effect is a carefully designed set. You need to build it so the actor is walking on the ground, but film it so it looks as if he isn't.

So to make a shot like this...

...you need to build a completely upside-down set like this...

Now turn the camera upside down and film the actor walking across the floor of the set. In the finished shot, she'll look as if she's walking on the ceiling.

The most famous effect of this kind ever done was in the movie *2001*, when a waitress walked right round the inside of a circular spaceship carrying a tray of drinks. She walked steadily the whole time and never spilled a drop, even when she was upside down. In case you haven't seen the movie, Eric has kindly shot a similar sequence showing Gloria taking her pet poodle, Fifi, for a walk in a spaceship.

Can you think how both sequences were filmed? (If you want a clue, think of a hamster in a wheel.)

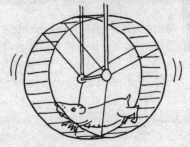

The answer is that each actor (and Fifi) walked on the spot while the specially designed spaceship set revolved around her. The camera revolved too at the same speed, so it looked as if she was moving while the set stayed still.

AMAZING DISAPPEARANCES

It's easy to make someone disappear in a movie. You just stop the camera, let them walk away and then start the camera again. When you play back the film, it looks as if they've mysteriously vanished into thin air.

Making someone disappear on stage is much more difficult, because the audience are watching all the time. But because it is so hard, they will be truly amazed if you manage to do it successfully.

Trap tricks

Some stages have a trapdoor – an opening in the floor big enough for someone to go through. If there is a lifting platform underneath which will lower very quickly, you can use it to make someone disappear before the audience's eyes.

Presto's second principle is important here. You'll need a bright flash or other distraction on stage to make people glance away briefly. You also need the trapdoor marked clearly on the floor so the actor who has to disappear stands in the right place.

If the actor needs more time to go down through the floor, you'll need something to completely hide her from view for a short time. Sometimes this can be part of the plot – the actor hears someone coming and hides behind a curtain or in a cupboard. Her pursuer searches for her unsuccessfully for a suitable length of time before opening her hiding place to reveal that she's disappeared.

IF YOU PROMISE NOT TO TELL ANYONE, I'LL LET YOU INTO A SECRET ... WHEN PRESTO PUTS SELINA THE DOWNRIGHT SKINNY INTO HIS MAGIC DISAPPEARING CABINET, SHE LIFTS THE FLOOR AND SLIPS AWAY THROUGH A TRAP IN THE STAGE WHILE THE DOOR IS SHUT

Gauze tricks

Another way to make someone disappear is with a lighting effect. Stand the actor behind a gauze curtain. If the light behind the curtain is brighter than the light in front of it, the audience will be able to see the actor easily. If you turn off the light behind the curtain and shine a bright light on it from the front, they won't be able to see through the gauze, so it will look as if both the actor and the area of the stage he was standing in have disappeared.

Mirror, mirror, on the wall...

You can use a variation on the gauze lighting trick to produce an amazing magic mirror. It uses an effect you can see every time you look out through your window at night. If the light is on in your room, it's hard to see outside, but you can see your reflection. If you turn your light out, your reflection disappears and you can see out easily.

The magic mirror is made of a sheet of ordinary glass or clear plastic set in a box. There's a light in the box behind the glass, but when it is off no light reaches the back of the glass at all, so if you shine a light on the front of it, the glass will act like a mirror. An actor can stand in front of it and the audience will see his reflection.

Now turn off the light at the front and switch on the light at the back. The reflection instantly disappears and the audience can see another actor standing behind the glass. Reverse the lighting again and the second actor disappears, replaced by the reflection.

Pepper's ghost

Sudden appearances and disappearances are particularly important in ghost stories and one way to do them is with a method developed by Professor Pepper in the nineteenth century. Just like the magic mirror, it needs some bright lights and a large sheet of glass or clear plastic, but this time the glass is not in a box. It's on the stage at an angle to the audience, but they don't notice it because they can see through it.

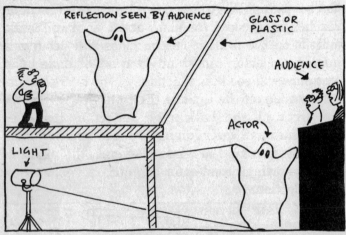

The actor playing the ghost stands in the wings close to the glass with a bright light pointing at her. While that light is off, she is in the dark and, because there is plenty of other light behind the glass, everything on stage will look completely normal. As soon as you turn on the light so it shines on the actor, the audience will see her reflection in the glass and it will look as if she is a ghost on the stage. If you turn the light off again, she will instantly disappear.

As she isn't really there, the other actors can walk through her just as if she was a real ghost. They can't see her at all so they need marks on the floor to show them where she is.

Invisibility

If you want one of your characters to become invisible rather than disappear completely, you will need to use special effects to give the impression that he is still there. On stage, most of those will involve string. You can use it to pull back chairs or lift spoons or move them around the room. Small puffs of compressed air can be useful too – they can turn the pages of a book and move the fringe on a lampshade to make it look as if someone is touching it.

Movie directors can be much more ambitious. An actor in an all-over blue bodysuit can walk around the set moving objects and then be painted out in post-production so no one can see him. He can even wear clothes over the blue suit so when he is painted out the clothes really look as if they are being worn by an invisible man.

A variation on this technique was used in *Forrest Gump* to make it look as if one of the characters had had his legs amputated. The actor wore blue stockings on his legs and these were painted out in post-production. Covering different parts of an actor's body can produce even stranger effects – a severed head hovering in the air and talking or a completely disembodied hand like Thing in *The Addams Family*.

Suppose you want one of your giant hamsters to become invisible and run across the snow leaving a trail of footprints. Instead of using computer graphics, you could use the same technique used in the 1933 version of *The Invisible Man*.

1. Dig a shallow trench and cover it with a piece of board.
2. Cut hamster footprints out of the board.
3. Push the cut-out pieces back into the holes and hold them in place with pegs. Tie a piece of string to each peg.
4. Cover the board with artificial snow.
5. Use the string to pull the pegs out one at a time. The cut-outs will fall down forming footprints in the snow just as if an invisible hamster was walking past.

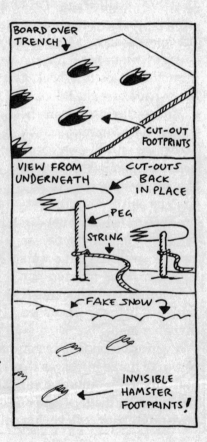

BOARD OVER TRENCH

CUT-OUT FOOTPRINTS

VIEW FROM UNDERNEATH

CUT-OUTS BACK IN PLACE

PEG

STRING

FAKE SNOW

INVISIBLE HAMSTER FOOTPRINTS!

SOUND EFFECTS

This chapter is at the end because, in movie making, that's when the sound effects are added. But that doesn't mean sound effects are less important than visual ones. Getting the sound right is a vital part of making special effects work. It's the sounds that make the audience believe the cardboard door is really a heavy iron one, the actor's feet are crunching through snow rather than foam and the computer-generated dinosaur is real enough to munch its lunch.

Making sounds

Some effects are added from pre-recorded sound tracks, but others are made in the sound studio in ingenious ways. You've probably heard of banging half coconut shells together to sound like horse's hooves but here are some others you may not have met before.

SLOBBERING DINOSAUR

SQUISH YOUR HAND AROUND INSIDE A MELON

RAIN

PEAS

SHAKE DRIED PEAS IN A JAR

CRACKLING FLAMES
CRUNCH PAPER OR PLASTIC

FOOTSTEPS IN SNOW
CRUSH CORNFLAKES

SOMEONE BEING PUNCHED
I HATE... "VEG!"
HIT HALF A CABBAGE

SWISHING SWORDS FOR A SWORDFIGHT
SWISH GARDEN CANES

Sounds aren't always used exactly as they were recorded. They are often changed electronically, blended together or even played backwards, especially when the sound team are trying to create noises no one has ever heard before. For instance, the Tardis materialization sound for *Dr Who* developed from the noise of a door key being scraped down piano wires, and the light sabre sound in *Star Wars* came from combining the hum from a microphone held close to a TV with the sound of a 35-mm film projector.

The noises for aliens, monsters and other creatures need to be realistic, so these are often based on recordings of real animals blended together and changed electronically. Speeding up the recording makes the sounds higher while slowing it down makes them deeper. The end result is usually very different to all the initial noises. When you listen to the screams of the raptors in *Jurassic Park* or the voice of Chewbacca, the wookie in *Star Wars*, it's hard to tell they were both based partly on the cries of walruses.

Mood music

The music in films helps put the audience in the right mood to believe what's happening on screen.

MY FIRST PRINCIPLE AGAIN!

High-pitched music can set nerves on edge and build a feeling of fear. Deep, ominous music suggests something dreadful is about to happen, while a heroic march accompanying the rescue party suggests everything is going to be all right.

In *Jaws*, Stephen Spielberg used the same piece of music repeatedly throughout the film when the shark was around. It started slowly with long, deep notes full of menace and became faster and faster as the shark prepared to attack. Whenever the audience heard that music, they expected a shark to appear. That meant they automatically assumed that any sudden movement on screen was one, even if they couldn't see it properly.

Very early movies didn't have sound but that didn't stop them using mood music. Every cinema had a pianist who played the music live for each performance.

SO YOU WANT TO WORK IN SPECIAL EFFECTS

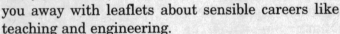

If you tell your careers teacher you want to work in special effects, he's likely to pull out what's left of his hair.

He's also likely to try to talk you out of it and send you away with leaflets about sensible careers like teaching and engineering.

The problem is there's no definite way into the special effects business. Most people who work in it started just like you. They were fascinated by effects in movies, watched them over and over until they worked out how they were done and tried to do them themselves at home. It was that enthusiasm and passion combined with hard work and practical skills which got them where they wanted to be.

So if you want to work in special effects, now is the time to start. Here's a few ideas from Eric, our resident FX man.

WATCH EFFECTS MOVIES OVER AND OVER UNTIL YOU CAN WORK OUT HOW THEY'RE DONE

REWIND◀◀

JOIN YOUR LOCAL AMATEUR DRAMATICS GROUP AND VOLUNTEER TO HELP BACKSTAGE

??

SNOW WHITE & THE SEVEN DWARFS

MAKE YOUR OWN MODELS AT HOME. START WITH KITS THEN LOOK FOR WAYS TO MAKE THEM BETTER AND START MAKING YOUR OWN FROM SCRATCH

GLUE

TRY EXPERIMENTING WITH CAMERA EFFECTS. YOU CAN USE A STILL CAMERA IF YOU HAVEN'T GOT A CAMCORDER

MY MOVIE

IF YOU CAN BORROW A VIDEO CAMERA, GET TOGETHER WITH SOME FRIENDS TO TRY MAKING YOUR OWN MOVIES

IF YOU HAVE ACCESS TO A COMPUTER, EXPLORE THE GRAPHICS SOFTWARE TO DISCOVER THE THINGS THAT YOU CAN DO WITH IT

GAME OVER

USE A TAPE RECORDER TO EXPERIMENT WITH SOUND EFFECTS ...

MIAOW?

LEARN AS MANY SKILLS AS YOU CAN: DRAWING, PAINTING, SCULPTING, SEWING, CARPENTRY AND METAL WORK ARE ALL USEFUL

TRY DESIGNING AND MAKING RADIO-CONTROLLED MODELS

EXPERIMENT WITH MAKING PUPPETS AT HOME

TRY PUTTING ON A PUPPET PLAY

Even if you change your mind and do something
else, you'll still have enjoyed yourself. But if you
persevere and work hard, you never know – one day
it could be you standing up in Hollywood to collect
an Oscar for Spectacular Special Effects.

EPILOGUE

Special effects have progressed enormously over the last 100 years and they are still changing. Movie writers and producers continue to push the boundaries of what is possible and computer graphics continue to improve. Soon we may be watching computer-generated actors in movies and adding computer-generated dinosaurs to our home videos.

But better technology doesn't mean the simple tricks won't work. Smoke will still build atmosphere and hide the dodgy scenery. Demon kings in pantomimes will still shoot up through trapdoors and magicians will still use Presto's three principles to make their tricks work. The fact we have the technology doesn't mean we always have to use it.

So what does the future hold? No one really knows. But one thing's for sure: the special effects are going to be spectacular.

THE END